ROYAL COMMISSION ON HISTORICAL MONUMENTS
ENGLAND

SUPPLEMENTARY SERIES: 3

EARLY INDUSTRIAL HOUSING

The Trinity Area of Frome

Roger Leech

LONDON HER MAJESTY'S STATIONERY OFFICE

© Crown copyright 1981
First published 1981
ISBN 0 11 700907 5

Published by Her Majesty's Stationery Office for
the Royal Commission on Historical Monuments
(England) in association with the Committee for
Rescue Archaeology in Avon, Gloucestershire and
Somerset.

EARLY INDUSTRIAL HOUSING

The Trinity Area of Frome

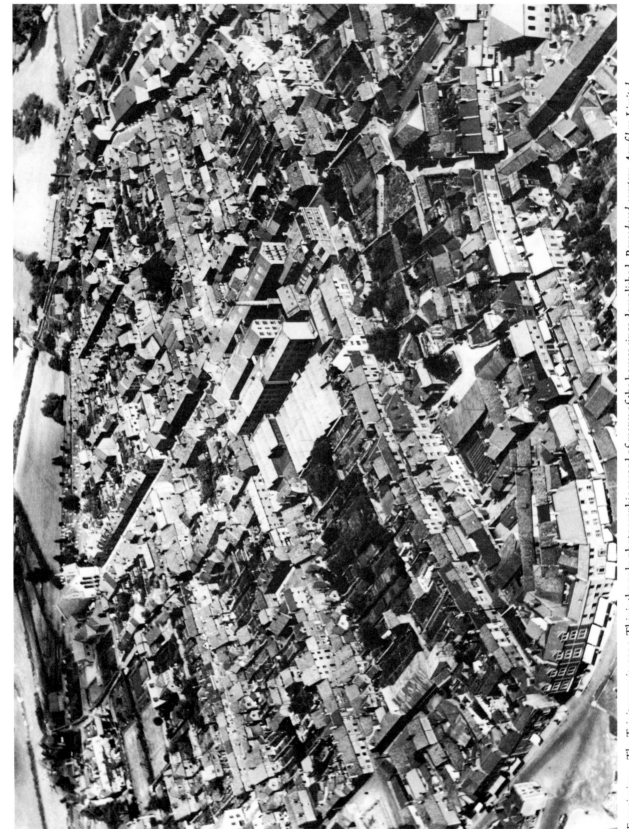

Frontispiece   The Trinity area in 1925. This is the only photographic record of many of the houses since demolished. *Reproduced courtesy Aerofilms Limited.*

CONTENTS

LIST OF ILLUSTRATIONS

ACKNOWLEDGEMENTS

My thanks are due first to the owners and occupiers of the houses of the Trinity area who have so willingly allowed the investigation of the property in their charge or ownership and especially to Mendip District Council and the Somerset County Council for their help in providing access to a large number of houses. Thanks are also due to the staff of the Public Record Office, the Somerset and Wiltshire Record Offices, and to various individuals who have permitted the examination of documents in their custody.

I am indebted to the Royal Commission on Historical Monuments (England) both for generous financial and other support and for the invaluable help and advice given by Mr E. Mercer and Mr R. W. McDowall at all stages in the preparation of this report and to Mrs G. Popper for her assistance in the editing of the final text; an equal debt is due to the Committee for Rescue Archaeology in Avon, Gloucestershire and Somerset for permitting the survey to be prepared under its auspices. I am especially grateful to Mr D. J. Gill of Frome, who has contributed greatly to the historical research and to the surveying of buildings and who wrote much of the historical introduction. Many other individuals and institutions have also been generous with their assistance, notably: Aerofilms Ltd; Mr M. Aston; Miss S. Collier; Mr P. Floyd; Dr P. J. Fowler; Frome Museum; Dr J. H. Harvey; Mr M. Jenner; Mr F. Kelly; Dr W. J. Rodwell, and finally, but with especial gratitude for their help and tolerance, Mrs Jean Gill and Mrs Pamela Leech.

The preparation of the plans was undertaken mainly by the author, but with assistance from the above and from members of the Frome Rescue Archaeology Group, Mr A. Elkan, Messrs Moxley Jenner and Partners, Mrs J. Richardson and Mr D. Hunter. The Frontispiece and Plate 20 are reproduced with the permission of Aerofilms Ltd and Somerset County Council respectively; all other photographs were taken by Mr Stephen Cole, Royal Commission on Historical Monuments and are Crown Copyright. Copies are deposited in the National Monuments Record.

ROGER LEECH

PREFACE

By the Chairman, the Rt. Hon. the Lord Adeane, PC, GCB, GCVO

In the summer of 1975, a large part of the Trinity area of Frome, Somerset, was threatened with the imminent demolition of many buildings. Only then was it realised that many of the houses formed part of an extensive urban development of the late 17th century. Preliminary research indicated that few, if any, urban estates of this period survived elsewhere, comparable examples in towns such as London and Manchester having been replaced by later redevelopment. Moreover, the first full-scale study recently published of 18th-century urban building in England had emphasised the lack of evidence about houses, and especially the smaller ones, of the early 18th century. In the present study attention has therefore been focused on the urban estate of the later 17th and early 18th centuries, a terminal date of 1813 being provided by Jeremiah Cruse's map of Frome. Nevertheless, occasional reference has been made to later developments where these were thought to be of interest.

ADEANE

COMMISSIONERS

The Right Honourable the Lord Adeane, PC, GCB, GCVO *(Chairman)*
Her Majesty's Lieutenant of Somerset *(ex officio)*
Sheppard Sunderland Frere, Esq., CBE
Richard John Copland Atkinson, Esq., CBE
George Zarnecki, Esq., CBE
John Kenneth Sinclair St Joseph, Esq., CBE
Paul Ashbee, Esq.
Arthur Richard Dufty, Esq., CBE
Mark Girouard, Esq.
Christopher Nugent Lawrence Brooke, Esq.
Andrew Colin Renfrew, Esq.
Irene Joan Thirsk
Peter Kidson, Esq.
Maurice Warwick Beresford, Esq.
Robert Angus Buchanan, Esq.
Albert Lionel Frederick Rivet, Esq.

Secretary
Peter Jon Fowler, Esq.

ABBREVIATIONS

JOL	Papers of the late Mr J. O. Lewis, Frome
Longleat MSS	Frome Manuscripts at Longleat House, Wilts.
MDC	Mendip District Council
NMR	National Monuments Record
PRO	Public Record Office
SCC	Somerset County Council
SRO	Somerset Record Office
WRO	Wiltshire Record Office

The plans and elevations of houses are at a scale of 1:250. Details are generally at 1:25. The following conventions are used in the illustrations:

Contemporary with or close in date to the initial construction of the building.

Later phases, but before 1813.

After 1813 or of uncertain date.

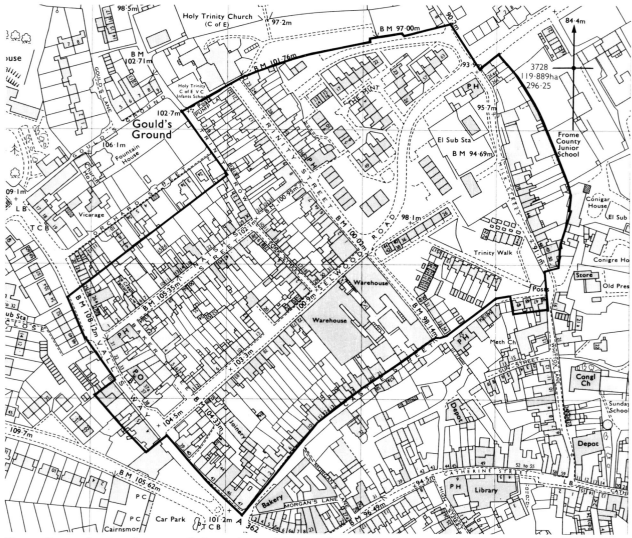

Fig. 1   Frome, showing the area studied. *Based upon the 1972 Ordnance Survey 1:2500 map.*

HISTORICAL INTRODUCTION

AREA STUDIED

In the last half of the 17th century, largely because of the prosperity of the cloth manufacturing industry, the town of Frome, Somerset, experienced a rapid increase in population. Between 1660 and 1695, the number of rateable inhabitants increased by at least four times (Church Rate Books, St John's Church, Frome). Daniel Defoe, writing in the early 1720s, compared the growth of Frome with that of Manchester, and recorded that 'The town of Froom . . . is so prodigiously increased within these last twenty or thirty years, that they have built a new church, and so many new streets of houses, and those houses are so full of inhabitants, that Frome is now reckoned to have more people in it, than the city of Bath, and some say, than even Salisbury itself, and if their trade continues to increase for a few years more, as it has done for those past, it is likely to be one of the greatest and wealthiest inland towns in England' (*A Tour Through the Whole Island of Great Britain* (Everyman Library, 1962), II, 280).

However, the rapid growth of Frome, so evident in the 1720s, did not continue beyond the 18th century.

The relative prosperity of the town declined in the 19th and early 20th centuries, and only since the 1950s has Frome again experienced a significant increase in population.

Much of the new housing provided in the late 17th and early 18th centuries was in the area which has since been named Trinity after the church built in 1837 in Trinity Street, similarly so named. The first reliable estimate of the population of the town as a whole, a survey of occupations of heads of households in Frome (Longleat MS, WMR Box 29), made for Lord Weymouth, shows that in 1785, out of a total of 8,125 persons, 2,084 lived in this area.

By the mid 20th century, housing conditions in parts of the Trinity area had deteriorated, particularly in those areas most subjected to 19th-century infilling. In the 1960s two successive redevelopment schemes involved the demolition of considerable numbers of houses. A third scheme was planned to begin in 1975, but this has now been replaced by proposals for rehabilitation of the remaining houses (MDC, *A report on the Trinity area, Frome, by Moxley, Jenner and Partners* (1978)).

The area studied in this survey encompasses both the streets redeveloped in the 1960s and those still remaining. The precise limits of the survey are shown in Figure 1 and are, approximately, Castle Street on the E, and the property boundaries behind Milk Street, Naish's Street and Vallis Way on the N, W, and S. In the text, streets are referred to by their existing or most recent names, with the exception of the N section of Selwood Road which for convenience is referred to by its older name of Broad Street. Appendix 3 lists street names past and present.

A wide variety of documentary sources has been of use in placing the buildings studied in their historical context. The classes of documents consulted are listed in Appendix 1, and to avoid an excessive number of references to individual houses all leases prior to 1800 are tabulated in Appendix 2.

TRINITY AREA BEFORE *circa* 1650

Fig. 2   Prior to development for housing, the area formed part of the fields to the W of the town. The field names indicate that they were formerly common fields, subsequently enclosed and given names such as Katherine Close, Mill Close, New Close and Selwood Close. The precise date of enclosure is uncertain, but is most likely to have been before the end of the 16th century (E. C. K. Gonner, *Common Land and Inclosure* (1912), 397–8). In the E corner of the area was the manor house of St Katherine's, some of which still remains, now called 'The Old Presbytery'. Architectural evidence indicates that parts are of the late 15th or early 16th century. Close by stood a dovecote, presumably in the field named 'Culver Close', and there was a rabbit warren in the field called 'Conigar' (PRO, C 2/Y2/11; Barnard Estate Act 1818, Private Act 58 Geo III cap. 30).

Before the Reformation, the manor house and most of the adjacent closes belonged to the free chapel of St Katherine. In 1548 the chapel was dissolved and its lands, including the manor house, were sold to Sir John Thynne of Longleat (*Calendar of Patent Rolls* 1548–9, 52). The lands then passed in 1563 to Richard West of Frome (Longleat MS NMR 5425) and later to his son, also Richard (PRO, Wards 7/53/193). In 1606 the estate, then over 75 acres in extent, was sold to West's uncle, John Yerbury of Atworth, for £400 (PRO, C 2/Y2/11). John Yerbury died in 1614, and it was his son Richard who first began to develop the Trinity area for housing (PRO, Prob. 11/8 Rudd/125).

DEVELOPMENT OF THE AREA FOR HOUSING

Fig. 2   By *c.*1665 houses had been built in the area of New Close. In the will of Richard Yerbury, dated to 1660, his property included 'four acres of pasture at Vallis Way . . . on the south side of a ground called "New Close" . . . with the houses thereon erected'; these probably included some of the twenty-six houses then 'part of St Katherines' (PRO, Prob. 11/119 May/305).

The boundaries of New Close can be accurately determined. In 1751 it was described as adjoining Mill Close and 'extending from Cross Street [now the E part of Trinity Street] to Vallis Way, containing several streets called Long Row [Castle Street], Long or Blount's Street [Selwood Road] and half a street leading from Mill Close to Vallis Way at the western end of the said close [Naish's Street]' (PRO, C 12/1812/5). The NW boundary lay on a line from the corner of The Globe Inn, no. 31 Vallis Way, to the NW end of York Street, and is discussed more fully below. The NE boundary was Cross Street, now Trinity Street, since leases for the E part of Trinity Street show that only the S side was included in New Close. The SE boundary was Castle Street, the way from St Katherine's Manor house to Badcox. Although some land on the E side of the same street was in the same ownership as New Close, it was probably a separate holding. The SW boundary was Vallis Way, for early leases for houses on the N side of Vallis Way usually refer to New Close, a typical one being that of 1726 for no. 38 which refers to the plot as being 'formerly in New Close; and adjoining the way from Frome to Vallis'.

The earliest houses in New Close, probably including most of those in existence by c.1665, were those on the N side of Vallis Way. Some houses in Castle Street could also be of this date but, significantly, the building at the N corner of Castle Street and Vallis Way fronts Vallis Way and not Castle Street, indicating that the former was built up first. The other streets in New Close will be shown below to have been built up at a later date. Selwood Road previously stopped short at the rear of the houses on the N side of Vallis Way; it can be argued that, when the latter was built up, the complex of streets which was to emerge later had not yet been envisaged. Moreover, the only reference to a lease of before 1679 is to one of 1667 for a house stated to be on the N side of Vallis Way and corresponding to a plot, no. 40A Vallis Way, later used to provide access to Baker Street.

By 1685 more extensive building had taken place and several new streets had been laid out. The owner- Fig. 2
ship of the closes being developed remained with the Yerbury family. The manor of St Katherine's had passed first in 1661 to Richard Yerbury II and then in 1672 to Richard Yerbury III, both of whom were absentee landlords (PRO, C 8/297/155).

By c.1685 within New Close the streets Castle, Trinity and York were being developed. A large house 'The Old Hospital', no. 23 Castle Street, at the corner of Castle Street and Trinity Street, has its main façade facing the former, indicating that Castle Street was developed first. Leases dated to 1679 refer to houses in Trinity Street and to no. 17 York Street, while a lease of 1688, referring back to three previous owners, refers to nos. 29, 30 and 31 Selwood Road. Nos. 1–3 Trinity Street form part of the same block and are thus of like date. No. 7 Trinity Street is also part of the same terrace, built in an E to W direction, and was constructed not much later than c.1679–80. Although not yet fully built up, the remaining part of Selwood Road was clearly planned by c.1685, since a break was left in the S frontage of Trinity Street and access provided to the houses in York Street.

By c.1685 the development of Mill Close had also begun. As with New Close, its limits can be accurately ascertained from documentary sources. In 1743, the boundaries of Mill Close were described as extending 'from the said capital messuage . . . called St Catherine's . . . to the north side of a street called Cross Street, and by the north east side of the said street to a close called Catherine Close, and by the said close to a place called Catherine Stile where formerly a stile stood, and from there to the said plot of ground called Lower Oad Ground, and by the said ground to the said manor' (PRO, C 12/1812/5). Cross Street is now part of Trinity Street, from nos. 1–7. The boundary on the NW thus extended from no. 7 Trinity Street to Milk Street. The NE boundary was Milk Street. On the SE side the boundary followed Castle Street. Properties on the E side of Castle Street were not in Mill Close, being in different ownership as early as the 18th century, for instance in 1753 when John Sedgefield sold No. 53 Castle Street and in 1829 when 'The Lamb and Fountain' was part of the estate of John Moon (deeds, MDC 362; Frome Museum D65). None of the properties there was listed in the 1753 survey of St Katherine's manor (Longleat MS, WMR Box 28).

The first part of Mill Close to be developed was probably the S side of Milk Street. A lease of 1686, not

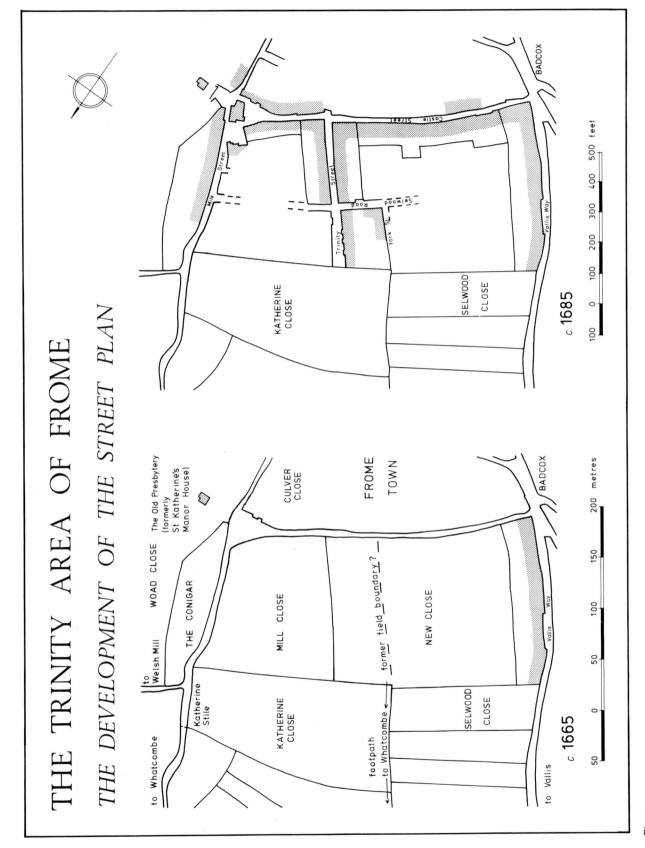

THE TRINITY AREA OF FROME
THE DEVELOPMENT OF THE STREET PLAN

Fig. 2

THE TRINITY AREA OF FROME

THE DEVELOPMENT OF THE STREET PLAN

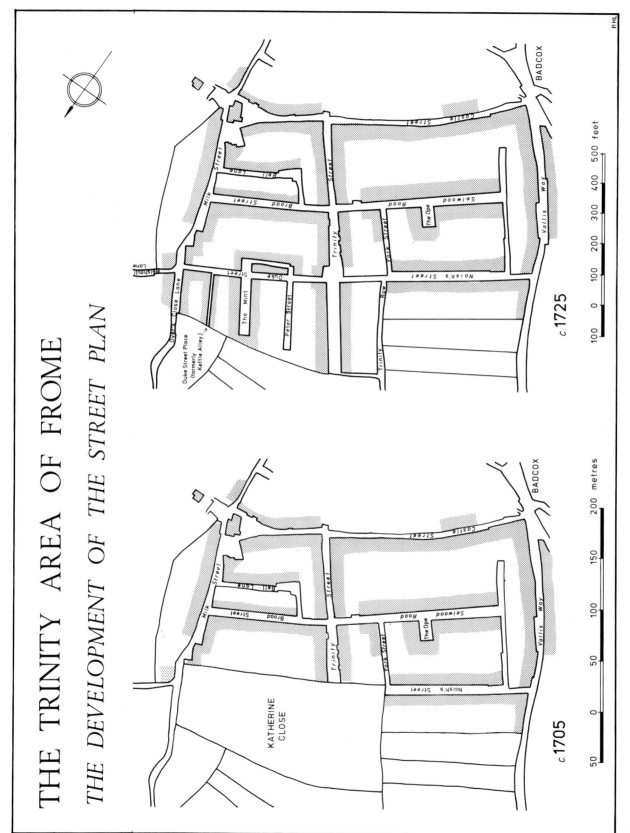

Fig. 3

accurately located, refers to the surrender of an earlier lease of a house and garden, roughly opposite the manor house. On the N side of Milk Street, in the close named The Conigar, development had also probably begun by c.1685. The boundaries of this close cannot be determined with complete accuracy but certainly included nos. 47–50 Milk Street. Although there are no early extant building leases for The Conigar, the plan-form and size of nos. 45 and 50 Milk Street are comparable to the early and largest houses in Vallis Way and on the S side of Trinity Street. However, the siting of larger houses in Milk Street could also be explained by the building of a more select development close to the manor house.

Fig. 3   By 1705 several new streets had been laid out and many more houses in existing streets built. In New Close, nos 7 and 8 Castle Street were being built in 1692; no. 67 Selwood Road was being constructed in 1695; and, further to the SW on the same street, no. 76 was built c.1699. On the W side of New Close, the development of Naish's Street was also begun in the 1690s; this was carried out jointly by Richard Yerbury III, the owner of New Close, and by John Selwood, the owner of the adjacent Selwood Close, Selwood contributing slightly more than half the total 30 foot width of the street. The E side of Naish's Street, in New Close, was developed from N to S, no. 40 being built about 1693. The W side was built up in the opposite direction; nos. 6/8 and no. 10 were being built in 1692 and 1693 respectively, but at the N end of the street nos. 29 and 30 were not constructed until 1705. The boundaries of Selwood Close, as shown on Figures 2 and 3, can be established both from the surviving leases for the 1690s and early 18th century, and from a sale catalogue of 1818 (in the possession of Mr J. A. Olive, Shawford House, Beckington, Somerset). The exact line of the ditch between the two closes is perpetuated by the W wall of no. 31 Vallis Way, constructed before Naish's Street was envisaged, and thus hard up against the boundary of Selwood Close.

The development of Mill Close was completed in the 1690s. The N side of Trinity Street was built up in an E to W direction, leases referring back to the original building dates of 1681, 1687 and 1692 (both nos. 42 and 43 Trinity Street). At the junction with Broad Street, the house plots were set out facing Trinity Street, indicating either that the latter was the more important or that it was built first. The development of Broad Street, was, however, of roughly similar date. On the E side, built up from N to S, the first house (nos. 9–11 Milk Street) on the corner with Milk Street was built in 1687. On the W side, building leases of 1689 and 1693 refer to properties which cannot now be specifically located.

A small proportion of Katherine Close lay on the SE side of Welshmill Lane at the N end of The Conigar and was also Yerbury land. This was developed by 1698, one dwelling, later no. 26 Milk Street, being built on a plot 54 feet wide.

Fig. 3   By 1725 the development of the street plan was more or less complete, the main part of Katherine Close having been laid out by Susannah Whitchurch for building between 1718 and 1723. Susannah's sister, Margaret, was married to Henry Bull of Frome, since 1705 the owner of the houses in Selwood Close. In 1723 Susannah married James Baily, a local apothecary, in whose family the ownership of the Katherine Close estate remained until the mid 19th century (early deeds for W part of Trinity Street nos. 8–9 inclusive, and The Mint, c.f. Appendix 2).

The boundaries of Katherine Close, like those of New and Mill Close, can be determined from documentary sources. The SW boundary was the footpath from Frome to Whatcombe, the width of Trinity Row being taken out of Katherine Close. The NW boundary was the present E boundary of Holy Trinity school, church and graveyard, extending to Dyers Close Lane; a lease for no. 23 Trinity Street, the last house in the terrace on the N side, refers to 'the close of John Allen being land formerly of Lionel Seaman' on the N and NW (PRO, Wards 7/53/193). Another lease, for nos. 12–15 The Mint, also mentions Allen's land on the N (PRO, C 2/Y2/1). The NE boundary was the S side of Dyers Close Lane and Milk Street, while on the SE the boundary coincided with the E sides of The Griffin Inn and no. 39 Trinity Street and with the W side of no. 7 Trinity Street.

The development of Katherine Close, apart from the parcel at the N end of The Conigar, began in 1718, both The Mint and the W end of Trinity Street being started in that year. Both were developed from

E to W and were completed by *c*.1723. The Mint and Trinity Street were 30 and 35 feet wide respectively; the back lanes to the properties, Peter Street and Duke Street Place (former Kettle Alley), to the N of The Mint, were 15 and 10 feet wide.

THE BUILDING PROCESS

The development of the Trinity area was promoted by the three principal owners, plots being leased for 99 years or for three named lives, whichever was the shorter. Leases were perhaps issued in blocks, for two surviving building leases for nos. 1 and 7 The Mint were both of 20 April 1719. The initial building lease was generally subject only to a yearly rent and to the condition that a house be built within one year, sometimes with a stipulation that it must be of the same height and depth as the house adjoining. Yearly rents varied considerably but were most commonly 2s. to 3s.; they were not increased at all between the late 17th century and at least 1753. Later renewals of a lease were subject to a fine, most commonly of 1 guinea in the early 18th century.

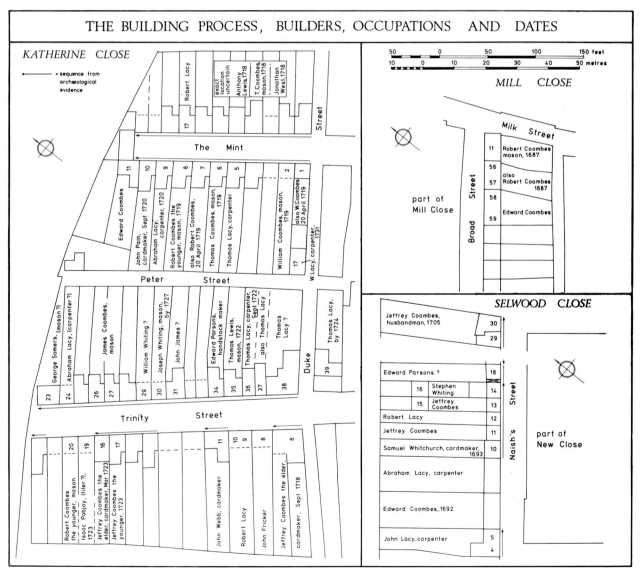

Fig. 4

Pl. 1

Fig. 4

Fig. 4

Fig. 4

The pattern of property boundaries on the 1813 and later maps indicates that blocks of house plots were successively set out for building. Thus, for instance, the W side of Castle Street was made up of several blocks of plots; the land between Selwood Road and Naish's Street consisted of four main parts. Possibly some of the streets and individual plot boundaries corresponded to alignments of ridge and furrow, no longer existing as field boundaries when the closes were developed but nevertheless still visible. Thus, in Katherine Close, it may be significant that many of the plots beyond the N side of Trinity Street followed the course of an inverted S-shape so characteristic of medieval ridge and furrow.

Much of the building was carried out by several families of tradesmen, of whom the Coombes's and the Whitings, mainly masons, and the Lacys, carpenters, were especially prominent. Naish's Street, built from 1692 to 1705, was actually known as Coombes' Street in leases of the early 18th century.

Other builders referred to in leases included more masons and carpenters, also helliers or tilers and a smaller number of persons in trades unrelated to building. In the surviving documents the names of the latter generally occurred only once or twice, for instance those of Samuel Whitchurch, cardmaker, builder of no. 10 Naish's Street in 1693, and John Pain, cardmaker, who built no. 10 The Mint in 1720.

Building-craftsmen sometimes retained their property as an investment; thus in the 1720s Thomas Lacy, carpenter, owned a group of houses at the junction of Duke Street and Trinity Street. Others mortgaged their houses fairly soon after they had been built, often defaulting later (SRO, DD/LW/81). Other builders, unrelated to the building trades, sometimes retained their houses to live in; for instance, the Pain family lived at no. 10 The Mint from its construction until after 1792. In some instances houses may have been built as an investment and sub-let; later leases and the 1753 survey reveal much evidence of sub-letting.

THE EIGHTEENTH AND EARLY NINETEENTH CENTURIES

The Yerbury and Whitchurch estates remained substantially intact until the 19th century. The former passed in 1736 to Daniel Yerbury, a nephew of Richard Yerbury III, and then to the latter's son, also Daniel, in 1741 (WRO, Sub-Dean of Sarum wills, 1736 No. 15). Thereafter, Daniel and his brother William fell into increasing financial difficulties and in 1756 the estate passed to Edward Barnard, the principal creditor (PRO, C 12/1812/5; PRO, C 33/40). After Barnard's death in 1807 the estate devolved upon four grand-daughters (PRO, Prob. 11/1460). To simplify the administration of the property, the Barnard Estate Act was passed in 1818; part, consisting of 128 lots, was then put up for auction in August of the same year (sales brochure, in the possession of Mr. J. A. Olive).

Between 1877 and 1887 the remainder of the estate was acquired by Edmund Ames, a solicitor of Frome. He purchased the various shares for a total of £2,775, and in two separate sales, on 23 March and 4 May 1887, the greater part was auctioned in forty-six lots (deeds, MDC 230, 520). For many houses the existing deeds begin with an abstract of title for that year.

Susannah Whitchurch's estate devolved in a similar manner, passing first in 1755 to her son William Baily (deeds, with Daniel and Cruttwell, marriage settlement of Wm. Baily) and then to his nephew William Hellier Baily, a shipcarver of Bristol. The latter died in 1834, bequeathing the estate to his six children. In the 1850s, two of their descendants, the Reverend F. E. Williams and his brother William, purchased the various shares for a total outlay of £969 (deeds of 87 Selwood Road, privately held). This investment was amply reimbursed, for, by a series of auctions, each house was sold and the estate broken up. Sales in 1878 alone, for which a record has been traced, totalled £1,800 (deeds for MDC properties in Trinity Street (W part) and the Mint, c.f. Appendix 2).

In contrast, the Selwood Close estate was broken up at a comparatively early date. In 1732 nos. 6–7 Naish's Street were sold to William Coombes, clothier, for £40, and no. 10 Naish's Street, a smaller house, was sold to John Whitchurch for £30. Other Selwood Close properties sold in the early 18th century probably included nos. 13, 14, 29 and 30 Naish's Street.

Throughout the 18th century there was variety in the pattern of ownership and tenancy. Some owners and chief tenants lived in their houses, but many sub-let, as is shown both by individual leases referring both to the lessee and occupier and by the repetition of certain lessees' names in the 1753 survey. The importance of house ownership as a means of investment to townsmen with modest sums of capital has been emphasised elsewhere (C. W. Chalkin, *The Provincial Towns of Georgian England* (1974)).

Of the leaseholders whose occupations could be identified, before 1813, 52% (56) were in trades associated with the cloth industry, for instance cardmakers, broadweavers and wiredrawers, 25% (27) were building-craftsmen while other trades accounted for 22% (24). However, the high proportion of persons associated with building derives from the tendency of lawyers drafting leases to refer back to the original leaseholder, often a building-craftsman. The figure of 52% is thus probably an underestimate of the proportion of the late 17th and 18th-century population of the Trinity area that was associated with the cloth trade.

Building continued sporadically throughout the 18th century, mainly in the gardens of houses built before 1725. For instance, nos. 52–55 Naish's Street were built by 1745; a house at the NE end of Peter Street, no. 17, was built in 1731 in the garden of a house built only twelve years earlier. At the corner of Welshmill Lane and Milk Street one dwelling was replaced by four before 1721. No. 6 York Street was built in the garden of no. 38 Naish's Street before 1813.

Cruse's map of Frome provides an exceedingly detailed and accurate delineation of the area in 1813. Pl. 1 There were houses built in most of those gardens which had rear access, while a number had been built in other gardens accessible only by alleyways, for instance behind both sides of Naish's Street. A very few houses had small areas at the street frontage, for instance nos. 7 and 11 Trinity Street and several houses in Milk Street. Most houses had privies at the backs of the gardens.

In the 19th century certain areas were even more intensively developed. Although houses of this period were not examined in detail, the following examples were among those noted and planned. Nos. 15–18 Selwood Road were built after 1813 infilling in the garden on the SW side of The Ope. Nos. 24–27 Selwood Road and no. 1 York Street form a terrace of 'blind-back' houses built in the garden of the house nos. 21–22 Selwood Road. Further, there were several instances of tenements in courts, behind houses fronting the streets, all of which are shown on the Ordnance Survey map of 1887. A typical instance was Cooke's Court 'otherwise the Barracks' behind Broad Street, consisting of four tenements around a rear courtyard (deeds, MDC 332). These have now all gone.

DEREK GILL
ROGER LEECH

THE SURVEY AND ITS RESULTS

THE SURVEY

The recording of the buildings was undertaken mainly in 1976. Altogether 137 houses were examined in detail, with plans being made of one or more floors; sections, elevations and details were recorded where appropriate. In almost all instances recording was by means of measured sketch-plans, always with diagonal measurements, transcribed at the earliest opportunity into accurately drawn plans at a scale of 1:50, all of which were later checked in the field. Much of the work was in very poorly lit, boarded-up, derelict houses.

Looting of derelict houses, particularly for pine cupboards and other fittings, began in 1976 and apparently took place on a large scale in 1977 and 1978. This eventually encompassed the removal of almost anything made of pine, such items as door architraves and boarded partitions being readily capable of transformation into stripped-pine furniture. Thus, in a number of houses, especially in Naish's Street, the plans made in 1976 were already inaccurate by 1978. At no. 19 Naish's Street the removal of pine panelling on the ground floor by looters actually caused the collapse of most of the house; they were Fig. 13 apparently unaware that the 19th-century rebuilding of no. 20 had resulted in the cross beams being supported largely on the pine-panelled partitions and that there was a wooden-floored cellar below, into which most of the house collapsed.

Figs. 5, 6 ## ANALYSIS OF PLAN-FORM

A plan common to all but a few of the houses built in the Trinity area between c.1660 and c.1720 consisted of a main ground-floor room, the hall, which had a street doorway at one end of the front wall, a doorway opposite the front door in the rear wall, a chimney stack against that side wall was further from the door-ways and a winder-stair against the stack, usually on the side away from the street. Often this main room was the only room on the ground floor, and houses of this form, usually of two storeys or two storeys and an attic, are designated A1 in the classification of plans set out in Figure 5. Other houses, however, had two ground-floor rooms from their inception; the hall as described above and another room, here called a parlour, which might be in line with the hall and lit from the street (A2 in the classification) or might be at the rear of the hall (A3). In the latter case the parlour was smaller than the hall in order to allow for the rear doorway of the hall. Occasionally there was a rear ground-floor room as well as a parlour on the street (A4). With one exception, at no. 45 Milk Street, this room was sited at the rear of the hall and not of the parlour, and, like the parlour in A3 houses, was shorter than the hall. In these A4 houses a rear doorway opposite the front doorway was not invariable.

Of the hundred or so A-type houses surviving, those occupying a street frontage of two rooms in width are few, about a score in all, that is, less than one-fifth of the total; the two variants of this type, A2 and A4, being equally common. Houses with a narrow one-room frontage, types A1 and A3, account for the other four-fifths. Of the two, A3 appears to be the commoner type, but, as explained below, this may be the result of later alterations and improvements to A1 houses.

As well as these A-type houses there are a few houses, about twenty in all, which have the stair not against the stack of the main room but in an external turret at the rear. This was patently a superior and more expensive way of building and it is not surprising that in these B-type houses, as they are classified in Figure 5, there are no B1 examples corresponding to the small A1 house. There are no B3 houses either, for it is not easy to site a stair-turret conveniently in a house two rooms deep. There are three surviving B2-type houses and all the rest are large houses with three rooms to a floor. Most of them are classified B4, corresponding to the A4 house, but three are classified B5. These three differ from every other house in the Trinity area in having the entry into a passage and not into a main room. Two of them, no. 23 Castle Street and no. 4 Vallis Way, have the added refinement of two heated rooms to a floor.

Among the houses built by c.1720, there were at the time of investigation only two exceptions to these plan-forms: no. 7 Castle Street, where the stairs were between the hall and the parlour, but this perhaps resulted from an early division of a larger house; no. 41 Naish's Street, where the stairs were approached from a small parlour. Possibly the unusual plan of the latter resulted from the house being constructed between two earlier buildings.

The plan-forms of classes A and B were all used within the context of continuous terraces, so that once the first house had been built the next could be added to the first by constructing two additional side walls and an end wall containing the second stack.

A few houses were built after c.1720 in the gardens of earlier houses. Most were of class A1, but with a framed winder-stair set opposite or at right angles to the stack as, for instance, at nos. 15–16 Naish's Street and nos. 1–2 Baker Street, both of 18th-century date, and at nos. 15–16 York Street and nos. 15–17 Selwood Road, all constructed in the early 19th century.

It is noticeable that the B-type houses and the larger A4-type houses tend to be concentrated in those parts of the area which appear to have been developed early, namely, Vallis Way, the eastern half of the S side of Trinity Street, and perhaps Milk Street. Conversely, they are almost entirely absent from parts which are known to be late developments, for example the western half of Trinity Street. This pattern suggests that, as happened later elsewhere, the development was originally meant to be select and to provide better accommodation than that which subsequently predominated in the area.

Fig. 6

	CLASSIFICATION BY BASIC PLAN				
	1 single room	2 hall and parlour against street	3 hall with parlour behind	4 hall and parlour against street with third room to rear	5 as 4, but with cross-passage
A stair against stack	57 Naish's Street	39 Naish's Street	74 Selwood Road	6 and 7 Vallis Way	
B stair in external projection		1 Castle Street		45 Milk Street	1 Trinity Street

CLASSIFICATION BY STAIRS POSITION

10 0 10 20 30 40 50 feet   5 0 5 10 15 20 25 metres   RHL

Fig. 5 Classification of plan-types (n. that plans are restored to their original form).

FUNCTION

Contemporary descriptions of houses and their rooms are almost entirely lacking owing to the wartime destruction of most wills and inventories in the Exeter Diocesan Registry. The only inventory relevant to the area is that of John Jelly, clothier, probably referring to the contents of his house in Vallis Way in 1724 (PRO, Prob. 4/24/42). The variety of rooms listed is applicable only to the larger houses: on the ground floor, 'a kitchen, little inner room, hall, pantry, cellar, brewhouse'; on the first floor, 'a best chamber, kitchen chamber and a little chamber'; above, 'the garrotts and wool loft'. The 'sheare shop' was presumably a separate building.

Where a house contained only one room on each floor, the ground floor was presumably the hall, with bed chambers above. In almost all the houses with two or three rooms, at least until the 1720s, the hall was the only heated room. Separate kitchens were noted only in a few instances, as at nos. 6–7 Trinity Street and no. 37 Vallis Way.

The uses of other unheated ground-floor rooms are a little more problematical. A smaller inner room was probably often used as a parlour, for instance at John Jelly's house, as indicated by the room's contents. In other cases, the unheated ground-floor rooms were probably used for cottage industries. Uses requiring good light are indicated by wide windows in a number of houses, for example at nos. 4–5 Naish's Street, Pl. 3 nos. 54–55 Naish's Street (inhabited by a broadweaver in 1745) and nos. 2–3 Trinity Street, which the 1813 map indicates had a circular dyehouse in the garden. Upper-floor rooms were also possibly used for cottage industry, but most were probably bed chambers as well.

ARCHITECTURAL STYLE

The houses built in the late 17th and early 18th centuries were generally of simple design, but with attention being paid to doorway and window details.

Pls. 6, 3   Well-proportioned, symmetrically designed façades were a characteristic feature of the larger houses, for instance, no. 23 Castle Street, nos. 5–9 Vallis Way and nos. 1–2 Trinity Street. Gables with attic windows were sometimes provided, usually in houses of two storeys and an attic; there are several examples Pl. 4   in Naish's Street, the latest being of c.1705. On the other hand, nos. 29–31 Selwood Road, built c.1679, were without attic gables and they are entirely absent from the W end of Trinity Street which was built Pl. 4   from c.1718. Houses originally of one storey with attic gables were recorded at no. 21 Castle Street, no. 19 Pl. 15   Selwood Road and nos. 12 and 13 Trinity Row.

Few original doorways have survived. Pedimented surrounds to those of no. 23 Castle Street, The Crown and Sceptre, The Bell Inn and no. 31 Trinity Street are possibly original.

Pl. 10   There was considerable variation in the types of windows used in houses up to c.1720. Smaller houses usually had stone windows of one to four lights in one height. Normally the mullions were chamfered, sometimes they were ovolo-moulded. A few wooden windows of similar style have survived. Out-buildings were sometimes provided with unglazed window frames having diamond-shaped wooden Pl. 16   mullions, as at no. 1 Trinity Street. The larger houses that are now nos. 5–9 Vallis Way, of c.1697, had four-light, mullioned and transomed windows of stone which, although not recorded elsewhere in the Trinity area, are a feature of larger 17th-century buildings in other parts of Frome. No. 23 Castle Street was the only house provided with bolection-moulded stone surrounds, for either casement or sash windows.

Original glazing was recorded in several instances, all in windows lighting stairs. Plain glass was set in diamond patterns within rectangular wooden frames at nos. 48 Castle Street and 39 Vallis Way. At no. 5 Pl. 16   Vallis Way, similar glazing within an oval surround was presumably a uniform feature of other stair windows in the same terrace. At no. 7 Trinity Street, one half of the decorative glazed fanlight, since looted, was a particularly fine survival.

The smaller number of buildings constructed in the later 18th century and the alterations to earlier ones

DISTRIBUTION OF PLAN TYPES

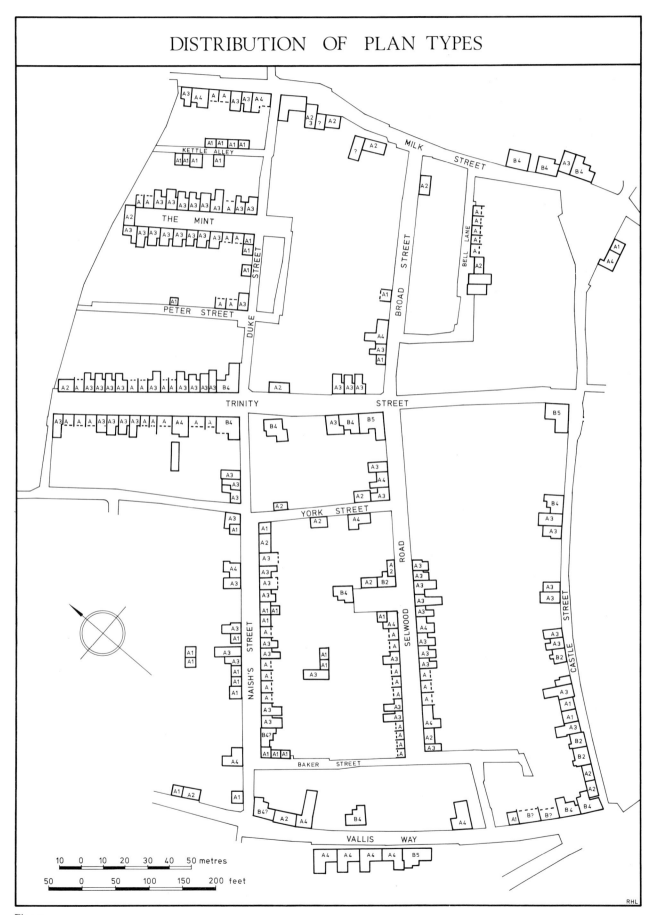

Fig. 6

provide evidence for changing architectural styles. Symmetrically planned façades of this period include examples at nos. 2–3 York Street and no. 45 Milk Street. Nos. 7–8, 10–11 and 12–13 Trinity Row are examples of smaller houses of simple design. In these and many other earlier houses there are numerous examples of both casement and sash windows.

In the 19th century the external appearance of many houses was altered by the insertion of larger windows and doorways together with heavy plain ashlar surrounds, which are characteristic of houses of Pl. 7 this period in Frome.

ALTERATIONS

Many of the 17th and early 18th-century houses were substantially added to or altered.

In the survey of smaller houses it was often impossible to be certain whether or not the rear wing was an addition, and some of those recorded as original may have been added, although probably only a few years after the first build. On the other hand, some additions were clearly later in date, including most of those which provided a rear range the same width as the front.

The original plan and construction of many of the smaller houses were well adapted to particular schemes of internal alteration. Partitions were easily and frequently added to create a through-passage separated from the hall. Fireplaces were inserted in the unheated rooms from the 18th century onwards, an early example being in the parlour of no. 19 Naish's Street. Kitchens were often added at the rear, for instance at no. 2 York Street and no. 10 Naish's Street. The winder-stairs were often altered; sometimes the last half-flight was removed and a new straight stair inserted so that access to the upper rooms was no longer from the hall but from a rear parlour, for instance, at nos. 10, 11 and 13 Naish's Street and nos. 10 and 11 Castle Street. More drastically, the stairs and the stack could be removed altogether, creating a considerably greater internal area. In the more complete alterations, both stack and floors were removed, making possible the raising of the attic to a full storey in height. This occurred at nos. 20–22 Selwood Road, which, after such substantial alterations between 1818 and 1831, were described as 'lately built' (deeds, MDC 540).

Windows were being altered as early as the first half of the 18th century, both to afford more light and accord with changing fashions. An early instance of the use of sash-windows is at no. 38 Naish's Street, but many other instances of the 18th and early 19th centuries could be cited.

CELLARS

Cellars were recorded in only a few houses, the first being that of c.1680 with a brick barrel-vault at no. Pl. 6 7 Trinity Street. Smaller stone barrel-vaulted cellars were noted in several houses, including nos. 10 and 39 Naish's Street, no. 11 Trinity Street and The Crown and Sceptre Inn, Trinity Street. Wooden floors over original cellars were recorded at no. 19 Naish's Street and no. 48 Castle Street.

INNS AND PUBLIC HOUSES

Several houses were probably built as inns although of the same plan-form as other larger houses. Inns recorded in the 1753 survey included The Star and Garter (probably no. 45 Milk Street), The Dolphin (probably nos. 62–63 Naish's Street) and 'The King's Head, late Whatleys Corner' (no. 1 Trinity Street). The Crown and Sceptre and The Bell were also probably built as inns. All have been much altered, but original brewhouses survive at The Bell and The King's Head.

BUILDING MATERIALS AND CONSTRUCTION

Before the mid 18th century the walls of almost all the buildings were constructed in coursed rubble. Exceptions were no. 3 Castle Street faced in ashlar, no. 23 Castle Street faced in brick, and no. 7 Trinity Street with a brick-vaulted cellar. Ground floors were paved in stone, upper floors and roofs were constructed of oak, at least until the 1720s, although pine or oak was used for doors from the 1690s. The joists of the upper floors were tenoned into the ceiling beams; possibly sometimes they were supported on oak wall-pads in the side walls, for these were noted at nos. 1 and 9 Castle Street where later alterations had been made. In the larger houses the attic floors were carried by the tie-beams of the roof trusses, the roofs themselves being of butt-purlin construction. The trusses were usually provided with collars, always morticed and tenoned into the principals. In smaller houses there were no roof trusses, the purlins generally being rough-hewn timbers running between the stone gable walls. Roofs were probably originally covered with stone tiles, surviving examples being recorded at no. 10 Castle Street and on the garden wall between nos. 22 and 23 Naish's Street.

Pl. 6
Pl. 6

Pl. 9

INTERIOR DECORATION AND FITTINGS

Stairs, ceiling beams, doorframes and doors comprise the greater number of surviving decorative features and fittings original to houses constructed up to *c*.1720. In the houses with winder-stairs there are numerous instances of moulded risers. Occasionally there are reeded mouldings on the newel and exceptionally, at no. 21 Castle Street, there is a moulded handrail to the top landing. In the larger houses with framed stairs, the risers are similarly moulded. The staircases at no. 45 Milk Street and no. 7 Trinity Street are particularly fine, having heavy turned balusters and chamfered newels, the latter formerly with ball finials.

Pl. 11
Pl. 11

In houses of before *c*.1705 doorframes to ground and sometimes first-floor rooms were often ovolo-moulded with ogee or plain stops. Those to attic-floor rooms were invariably plainer. Sometimes door-frames of that period were moulded on the exterior face only, or had applied mouldings, a practice which had become general by the 1720s. Comparison may be made between the earliest recorded examples, for instance at nos. 37 and 39 Vallis Way, with those in Selwood Road and Naish's Street of the 1690s and in the W end of Trinity Street of 1718–23. Ceiling beams were at first deep and deeply chamfered, generally with bold ogee stops, becoming by the 1690s both wider and shallower. Latterly a slighter ogee stop was occasionally used, the stepped plain stop was then far more common, coming into exclusive use by the 1720s. No ovolo-moulded ceiling beams were noted.

A few original exterior oak doors survive. These are of plank-and-batten construction, plain as at no. 45 Milk Street (cellar level), with covering strips as at no. 39 Naish's Street and studded as at no. 7 Trinity Street. Original internal doors are more numerous. Oak doors were in a variety of forms but generally with reeded mouldings on the stiles and rails, as at nos. 1 Trinity Street, 1 Castle Street, 4 Vallis Way and 45 Milk Street. A plank-and-batten door, studded and with three panels at no. 31 Selwood Road was very unusual. Other doors from the 1690s onwards were in pine and usually either panelled in two heights or were of plank-and-batten construction. Panelled doors demonstrably *in situ* were those to the stairs in no. 5 Naish's Street and no. 78 Selwood Road.

Pl. 12

Pl. 12

A number of original hinges were noted, plain or decorated, H and L types being the most numerous. There were particularly fine shaped hinges to the attic doors of no. 45 Milk Street.

Pl. 17

Panelling was rarely used for wall-lining, the only recorded examples being at no. 45 Milk Street and no. 19 Naish's Street, both early 18th-century insertions. Reset panelling was noted in nos. 54–55 Naish's Street. The only example of a plank-and-muntin partition was from no. 53 Naish's Street. Plaster was the commonest covering for walls from the later 17th century onwards. One instance is known with painted decoration, namely, in a house in Broad Street where two paintings, both subsequently whitewashed, were discovered in the late 19th century; one had 'in the centre of a wooded glen . . . a fawn dancing to music

Pl. 17

played by another fawn on a double flute reclining on the grass on the right-hand corner of the picture. On either side of the musician is a recumbent nymph. In the background are some trees and a mountain reaching to the skyline. The size of the picture . . . is 3 feet 4 inches square and the painting is surrounded with a black band in lieu of a frame'. To the left was a second picture showing a coat of arms; the crest had 'a castle over a helmet, and, below, armorial bearings in red, with three other castles, . . . the words "In the Lord is our trust" ' and the date 1693 (Frome Museum, newspaper cuttings).

Pl. 17 Recessed corner-cupboards with arched niches and shaped shelves were recorded in three houses; at nos. 45 Milk Street, 20 Selwood Road and 19 Naish's Street. All were later insertions.

Pls. 8, 13 Many original large open fireplaces were noted, more remain concealed by later blockings. Most ground-floor fireplace openings had oak bressumers, sometimes with a stone inglenook to one side. More elaborate chimney-pieces were recorded at no. 20 Selwood Road, where a panelled bolection-moulded fireplace surround was probably *in situ*, and at no. 1 Trinity Street, where an ovolo-moulded stone surround with a brick-faced fireback was exposed during survey. Other examples of brick-faced fire-backs have been recorded elsewhere in Frome, for instance at no. 13 Bath Street and no. 26 Vicarage Street where three triangular stones, two bearing the date and the third the initials of the owner, were set above the brick facing; matrices for similar stones were noted at no. 1 Trinity Street. The triangular date-stone from the fireplace at no. 39 Vallis Way clearly came from a similar fireback. On upper floors, a number of simple iron grates were possibly original. An elaborate stone chimney-piece with a fluted keystone to an ogee arch on the first floor of no. 2 Trinity Street, built *c.*1680, may be original. Similar examples have been recorded at a house in Guinea Street, Bristol, built *c.*1718, and at Downend Park Farm, Avon, both associated with Delft tiles of the early 18th century (RCHM MS files, Bristol, Avon).

Pl. 13

Pl. 13

Pl. 14

Pl. 14

URBAN DESIGN

Evidence that the three main parts of the Trinity area were planned as urban developments came not only from the history of the individual estates but also from the layout of the streets and properties.

Pl. 2 All the streets were lined with blocks of terraced houses. The earliest, in Vallis Way and, possibly, Castle Street, are of varying depth and perhaps predate a time in which uniformity became a basic principle of urban design. The remaining streets all exhibit a considerable degree of uniformity. Nos. 1–7 Trinity Street probably made a continuous terrace, the front range being of a constant depth. Selwood Road and Naish's Street each consists of several separately conceived terraces. The W end of Trinity Street is the most uniform, consisting of just two terraces of almost constant depth.

Pl. 18

Pl. 3

Pls. 18, 19

In some of these terraces, there is evidence that the houses themselves were of uniform appearance, particularly nos. 5–9 Vallis Way, the E side of Selwood Road, both sides of Naish's Street and the W end of Trinity Street. In the last, there is a continuous string-course between the ground and first floors.

Pls. 18, 19

The very few building leases that survive indicate that houses were intended to be uniform in appearance. In 1693 no. 10 Naish's Street was to be built 'the full width of the ground and the same height and breadth of the house . . . adjoining'. In 1705 nos. 29 and 30 Naish's Street were to be built 'equal in height with the other building there built'.

Behind the various terraces of houses were regularly laid-out gardens bounded by stone walls, many of which still survive. The properties fronting streets laid out from *c.*1679 formed the most uniform blocks; in New Close and Mill Close these were parts of a larger plan, the principal feature of which was the cross formed by the intersection of Selwood Road/Broad Street and Trinity Street. The three back lanes, Bell Lane, Baker Street and York Street, were also part of this plan, as was the small square known as The Ope.

The most carefully planned development was in Katherine Close where there were six parallel streets. In Trinity Street, in The Mint and on the S side of Milk Street the principal terraces fronted on wide streets. Trinity Row, Duke Street Place (former Kettle Alley) and Peter Street were of lesser width, being back lanes to the gardens and to some of the cottages built there.

URBAN DEVELOPMENTS ELSEWHERE   Fig. 7

The buildings of the Trinity area of Frome were probably typical of many developments in towns else-where in the late 17th and early 18th centuries. Close at hand in Shepton Mallet, Somerset, houses similar in date and plan to those of classes A and B have been recorded within the context of urban terraces (RCHM MS files, Shepton Mallet, Somerset). In Bristol some of the smaller urban terraces built in the early 18th century also included houses of similar plan. No. 17 Wade Street, part of an estate developed between 1700 and 1720, consisted of one room on each floor with the winder-stair against the stack. No. 82 Hotwell Road, a little later in date, had the winder-stair opposite the stack, a change in layout noted also in Frome (RCHM MS files, Bristol, Avon).

In Dudley, Worcestershire, some recently recorded town houses of c.1703 may be usefully compared with the larger houses of the Trinity area, for instance nos. 1–7 Trinity Street and the S side of Vallis Way, Frome, with nos. 6 and 7 Priory Street, Dudley. Each corresponded to class B4, with external stair pro-jections, three or more rooms on each floor but with entrance from the street originally into the hall. As

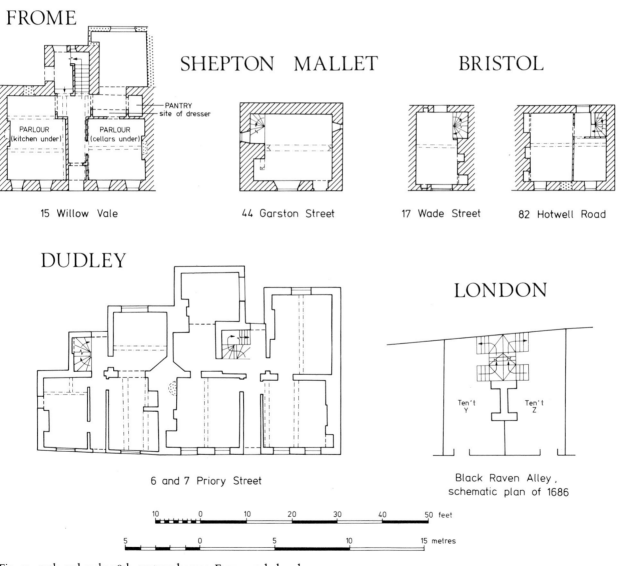

FROME

SHEPTON MALLET

BRISTOL

—PANTRY
site of dresser

PARLOUR
(kitchen under)

PARLOUR
(cellars under)

15 Willow Vale

44 Garston Street

17 Wade Street

82 Hotwell Road

DUDLEY

LONDON

Ten't Y   Ten't Z

6 and 7 Priory Street

Black Raven Alley,
schematic plan of 1686

10   0   10   20   30   40   50 feet

5   0   5   10   15 metres

Fig. 7   17th and early 18th-century houses, Frome and elsewhere.

with some of the Frome examples, the front cells were of uniform depth, whereas to the rear the various rooms interlocked in a complex manner (RCHM MS files, Dudley, West Midlands).

In London, where many houses were built in the closing decades of the 17th century, only a minute number of the smallest survive although the plans of others can be obtained from plan books. The long-demolished houses in Black Raven Alley were similar to those noted in Frome and Bristol, consisting basically of one room with a winder-stair against the stack (B. Hobley and J. Schofield, 'Excavations in the City of London,' *Antiquaries Journal*, LVII (1977), fig. 7). Of the few surviving examples, nos. 19–20 Cock Lane, St Bartholomew's, are of similar plan-form but have winder-stairs opposite the stack (information from Historic Buildings Section, Greater London Council).

Possibly the most extensively recorded examples of 17th-century urban development are the houses of the Rows, Great Yarmouth. The plans of the majority of these can be compared with the class A1 houses of the Trinity area, thus having one room on each floor and a winder-stair against the stack in the gable-end wall. Each row of houses was built as a terrace to a constant depth, with later additions to the rear forming a more complex pattern of development.

An important difference between the houses of Great Yarmouth and those of the Trinity area was that in the former, entrance was usually into a through-passage. However, most of the Great Yarmouth houses were of the first half of the 17th century. Only in the latest, after *c.*1650, was entrance directly into the ground-floor room as was almost always the plan in the houses of the Trinity area (B. St J. O'Neil, 'Some Seventeenth-Century Houses in Great Yarmouth', *Archaeologia*, XCV (1953), 141–80).

Common to all the houses discussed above was the fact that only the part fronting the street occupied the full width of the plot. If the builder so wished, the plan could consist merely of a single room on each floor. These plan-forms were probably typical of the smaller houses being constructed in the 17th and early 18th centuries on the outskirts of towns and elsewhere where circumstances were favourable. However, in developments in the centres of the more important towns, tenements two rooms in depth, often of four stories and occupying the full width of the plot were being built; in London in the 16th century, for example nos. 63–65 Grays Inn Lane, dated to 1595 but now demolished (Bristol Record Office, BMC/12/PL4/68). Closer to Frome, in 17th-century Bristol, where they were commonplace, surviving examples include nos. 3–5 King Street and nos. 35–41 Old Market.

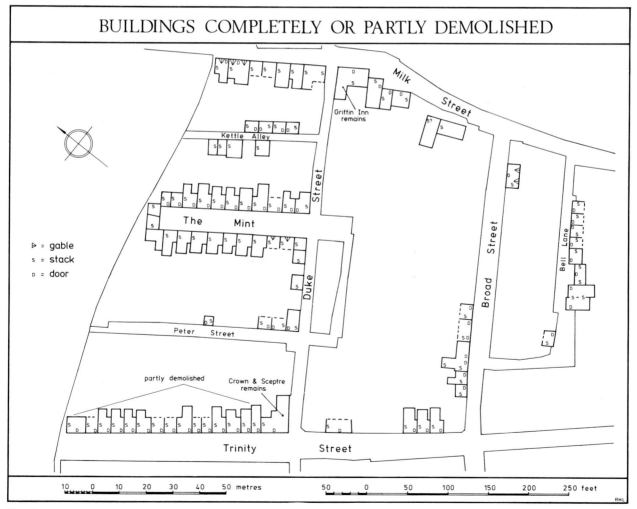19

DESCRIPTION OF INDIVIDUAL HOUSES

HOUSES COMPLETELY OR PARTLY DEMOLISHED

Part of the Trinity area development was demolished in the 1960s when many of the buildings were thought to be of 19th-century date. At that time no records were made of these houses. Nevertheless, from records made for other purposes, it has been possible to reconstruct the appearance and form of many of the demolished houses. Air photographs were particularly informative. They included an early and exceptionally clear oblique photograph of 1925 (Frontispiece) and vertical photographs taken by BKS Pl. 20 Surveys, their usefulness being all the greater because of the almost complete absence of any ground level photographs; the few that existed were of Bell Lane, part of Milk Street and part of Trinity Street (Frome Museum). Photographs of the N side of Trinity Street had been taken by the District Council before restoration and part demolition. These, used in conjunction with plans and elevations made at the time, yielded much information (MDC, Technical Services Dept., Frome).

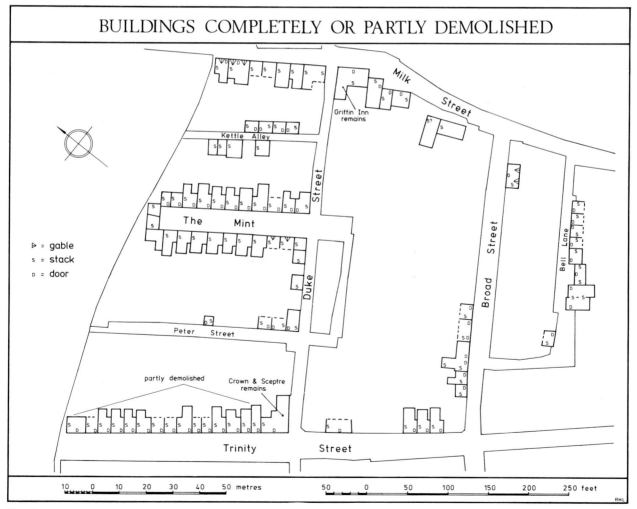

Fig. 8

From these diverse sources it would be possible, although not attempted here, to reconstruct parts of the plans and elevations of many of the demolished houses. Most useful was the information relating to the positions of doors, stacks and rear cross-wings. Plotting these enabled a tentative assessment of the various plan-forms to be made. In The Mint the evidence clearly indicated that, as in the W end of Trinity Street, building proceeded from E to W.

Figs. 4, 8

HOUSES SURVEYED

This section is a descriptive synthesis of the 137 houses surveyed in detail; it includes only those of which plans are here published. Fuller accounts of all the houses are deposited in the National Monuments Record. Houses were built of coursed rubble unless indicated otherwise. The classes of plans referred to are those set out below.

Fig. 9	CASTLE STREET (E SIDE)

CASTLE STREET (E SIDE)

No. 48, 17th century, of A1 plan, with two storeys, a cellar and an attic, abutting no. 49 and occupying a plot 17½ft wide. Against the stack in the N end-wall is a winder-stair with moulded risers; a window to the street is now blocked. The axial ceiling-beam to the ground floor is chamfered with stepped plain stops. The front cell is later, perhaps of the early 18th century, the first floor being constructed of brick with timber framing, similar to the first-floor extension to no. 30 Selwood Road.

Pl. 2

No. 49, 17th century, of A4 plan, with two storeys, a cellar and an attic, possibly abutting no. 50 (demolished). There are two main cells on an L-shaped plan. Several windows to the front elevation are original, having ovolo-moulded wooden frames. The attic is lit at the rear by two three-light windows. The principal range contains the hall and an unheated parlour now separated by a brick partition (omitted on the plan), the position of an earlier partition being indicated by stepped plain stops to the axial ceiling-beam. The stack is against the N end-wall; the original fireplace opening survives, partly unblocked, and has a stone inglenook seat, ashlar jambs and an unchamfered oak bressumer. The winder-stairs have moulded risers and are lit by a small window. The first floor consists of two rooms, the doorframe between them being ovolo-moulded with stepped plain stops. The gabled unheated cross-wing to the street side is contemporary or possibly an early addition, perhaps a shop with a room above. The roofs are of butt-purlin construction, that to the principal range dividing the attic floor into two bays.

Pls. 2, 7, 10

CASTLE STREET (W SIDE)

Fig. 9, Pl. 18

House 'B', late 17th century, one of a pair of dwellings, occupying a plot 55ft wide. Originally of A1 plan, it has been completely altered internally and is now a woodworking shop; the recess for a winder-stair is in the NW corner.

Nos. 1 and 2, late 17th century, pair of dwellings, of two storeys and an attic; each of an identical plan of class B2, together occupying a plot 50ft wide. Both have been much altered in the 19th and 20th centuries. The ground floor consisted of an unheated parlour and the hall, entered directly from the street. There was probably an axial ceiling-beam (removed from both) which was tenoned into the cross beam, which survives in no. 2, and which probably corresponds to the division between hall and parlour; in no. 1 a now redundant principal rafter at attic floor-level is on this same alignment. The winder-stair was contained in a small gabled projection, lit by a window with a chamfered wooden frame. On the first floor of no. 1 is a repositioned 17th or early 18th-century door with four raised fielded panels in three heights.

No. 3, late 17th century, built of ashlar, abutting and later than no. 2, of two storeys and an attic, and of A3 plan. Together with nos. 4 and 5, it occupies a plot 55ft wide (see house 'B'). The dwelling was much altered internally in the early 19th century, and all the door furniture and the ground-floor chimney-piece are of that date. The roof is carried on rough-hewn purlins between the gable walls. The rear cross-wing is probably contemporary with the front range, and was

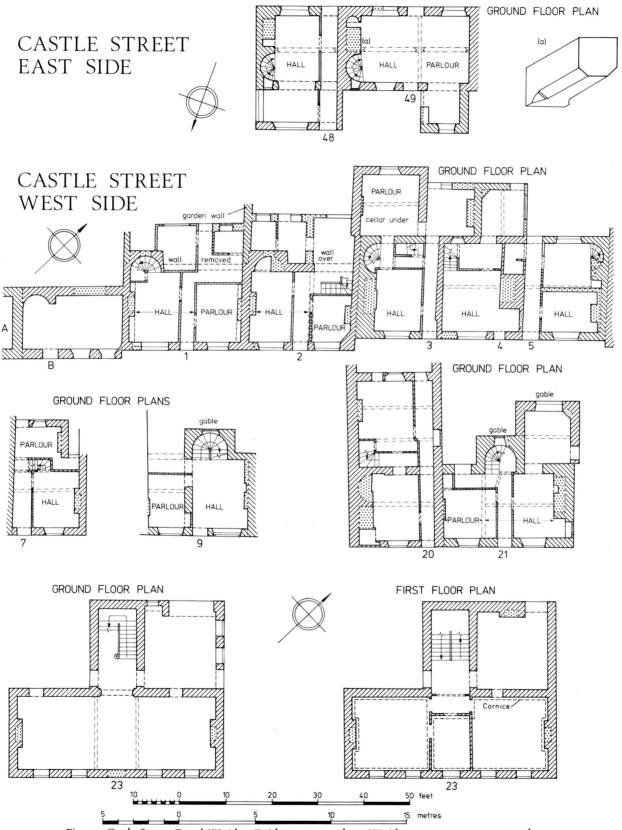

21

CASTLE STREET
EAST SIDE

GROUND FLOOR PLAN

HALL   HALL   PARLOUR

49

48

(a)

CASTLE STREET
WEST SIDE

garden wall

GROUND FLOOR PLAN

PARLOUR

cellar under

wall   removed
wall
over

HALL   PARLOUR   HALL
PARLOUR

HALL   HALL   HALL

A

B

1   2

3   4   5

GROUND FLOOR PLANS

PARLOUR

HALL

gable

PARLOUR   HALL

7   9

GROUND FLOOR PLAN

gable

gable

PARLOUR   HALL

20   21

GROUND FLOOR PLAN

FIRST FLOOR PLAN

Cornice

23   23

10   0   10   20   30   40   50 feet
5   0   5   10   15 metres

Fig. 9   Castle Street, E and W sides. E side, nos. 48 and 49. W side, nos. 1–5, 7, 9, 20, 21 and 23.

originally unheated, the ground floor being converted into a living room in the early 19th century with the addition of shutters and glazed panelled doors to the garden. The roof to the rear is of butt-purlin construction with one closed truss and with the purlins set into the rear wall of the main range which is built up as a gable, as at no. 39 Vallis Way.

No. 4, late 17th century, of A1 plan, of two storeys and an attic, now consisting of two main cells. The front cell probably contained one room on each floor with a winder-stair against the stack. The original stairs and entrance were possibly removed when nos. 4 and 5 were converted at an unknown date into one house. A straight joint in the rear elevation shows clearly that they were built separately. On the ground floor, there is an 18th-century chimney-piece with moulded surround and mantelshelf; the axial ceiling-beam is chamfered with stepped plain stops. The single-storey rear cell consists of one room with a rough-hewn ceiling-beam and a lean-to roof, and is probably of 18th-century date.

No. 5, late 17th century, of A1 plan, with two storeys and an attic, now divided into two main cells; the original plan probably consisted of one room on each floor with the winder-stair against the stack in the N end-wall. On the ground floor, the stack has been partly removed, the sequence of earlier blockings being visible in the side of the cupboard in the rear room. The former line of the stack is indicated by the position of the N stop to the chamfered axial ceiling-beam. On the first floor, there is an original door to the stairs which were lit by a window, blocked, in the N attic gable-wall. The roof is of butt-purlin construction with one open truss. Both on the ground and attic floors there are blocked doorways to no. 4.

No. 7, c.1695(?), of two storeys and a loft, occupying a plot 16ft wide. The plan is unusual and possibly results from the earlier division of a larger house into nos. 7 and 8, the latter completely rebuilt in the 19th century. Deeds and the 1753 survey indicate that nos. 7 and 8 together comprised the house built by Theophilus Crease, hellier, in 1695.

The ground-floor plan of no. 7 consists of three main cells: the hall, stairs and an originally unheated cross-wing to the rear. The hall was formerly entered from the street, the partition between it and the passage being of 19th-century date. The framed staircase, with moulded risers, is probably not later than c.1700–20. The first floor is carried on two axial beams; the doorframe to the front room is ovolo-moulded with ogee stops. The loft to the rear cross-wing has an original louvre window.

No. 9, late 17th century, of B2 plan with two storeys. It was partly altered in the 19th century, when the axial ceiling-beam was removed and the range was raised in height and refenestrated. In the hall, the original fireplace has been removed; in the formerly unheated parlour, the axial ceiling-beam is chamfered with stepped plain stops. A small gabled cross-wing to the rear contains the winder-stair.

No. 20, late 17th century, of A3 plan, cement rendered, with two storeys and an attic. The front attic window has much-weathered mullions with a hood-mould. The thick wall between the front and rear cells indicates that when building commenced, a plan of class A1 was intended. As completed, the building consisted of two cells, for the roof, of butt-purlin construction, is at right angles to the street and is of one build throughout. The two cells formed one dwelling, for in the closed truss between the front and rear parts is an original doorframe, chamfered with ogee stops. Moreover, the rear part of the house was originally unheated. The ground-floor plan thus consisted of the hall, entered from the street, and an unheated parlour and side passage to the rear. The rear beam is chamfered with stops, indicating that the partition between the two is original.

At a later date, the building was divided to form separate dwellings. The original entrance then led into a passage to the rear part, while the hall was entered from beside the stack through what is now a recess in the front wall. The framed stair in the rear cell was probably added at the time of this division. In recent times, the house has again been one dwelling.

No. 21, late 17th century. A dwelling of B2 plan, originally with one storey and an attic and with gables to the street elevation. Its structural relationship to no. 20 is uncertain. Entrance was into the hall giving access to an unheated parlour and the stairs. The stack is in the N wall. The axial and cross ceiling-beams are cased; there are moulded risers to the stairs. On the first floor, the stair handrail is shaped and moulded; the doorframes to the two front chambers are ovolo-moulded with ogee tops. There is a loft with a blocked slit window in the gabled roof over the stairs. The gabled cross-wing to the rear was added afterwards. There is a cased ceiling-beam to the ground floor; the rear window to the first floor has a stone hood-mould. Pl. 11

No. 23, 'The Old Hospital', c.1720, of B5 plan with two storeys and an attic. Both W and S façades face on to streets. The main, W, façade is of brick with stone dressings, the door and window frames are moulded. The side walls are of stone. All details suggest a date c.1720.

The house is L-shaped in plan and originally had a central entrance-hall flanked by reception rooms, with stair hall and kitchen with its own external entrance and large fireplace, in the rear wing. No details survive on the ground floor. On the first floor, fragments of original cornice remain at the front, indicating that a small central lobby gave access to a square and an L-shaped room. About 1800 the staircase and stair hall were remodelled. The staircase has a swept handrail, spindly balusters and turned newel. There are modillion cornices to the ground and first-floor stair halls. At a later date the front range of the first floor was divided into three rooms. In the late 19th century the ground-floor rooms were given new fireplaces and cornices. The attic was formerly lit by gable windows, but dormers were inserted and the parapet built up to hide them.

In the polite nature of its architecture in an area exclusively vernacular, in its use of brick and in the classical character of its ornament, this house is unique in Trinity. Also noteworthy is the building c.1720 of so well-appointed a house in an area which by that time contained houses of a poorer quality, an area which in fact had been largely built up by c.1705.

Pl. 6

Fig. 10

MILK STREET (N SIDE)

No. 45, Lewis Cockey's 'Bellhouse', late 17th century, of B4 plan with two storeys, a cellar and attic, the original plan being L-shaped with three main cells. The street elevation was rebuilt in the late 18th century.

The principal range is entered by a cross-passage, giving access to the parlour, hall and stairs. The parlour was not certainly heated and has raised fielded panelling in two heights; it is of early 18th-century date, as is also the recessed cupboard with shaped shelves against the stack in the E end-wall of the hall. The blocked door to no. 46 is of 19th-century date. The cased axial and cross ceiling-beams to the ground floor indicate that in the original plan entrance was directly into the hall. If a cross-passage had been part of the original plan, the arrangement of ceiling beams would probably have followed the pattern of those in 15 Willow Vale, Frome, a contemporary house of similar size.

Fig. 7

Two gabled cross-wings to the rear contain what was possibly a third unheated room and the staircase; the latter has moulded risers, closed strings, turned balusters, chamfered newels with plain stops and a moulded handrail. At attic level the balusters are framed in panelling.

Many other early features survive. At cellar level these include an exterior door and ovolo-moulded and chamfered wooden window-frames; on the first floor, a cupboard against the stack has two doors, each with three fielded panels in two heights. On the attic landing, the doorframes are chamfered with plain stops; the doors are each of two panels with moulded stiles and rails and shaped hinges. The roof is of butt-purlin construction.

The gabled cross-wing to the NE is a later addition, but is not later than the early 18th century and must be contemporary with the rear cell of no. 46.

Pls. 5, 12, 17

No. 50, late 17th century, of B4 plan with two storeys, an attic and cellar. Of similar plan to no. 45, but now converted into two flats and very much altered. Surviving features included ceiling beams, cased, and the staircase.

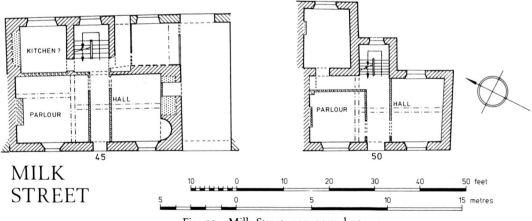

MILK STREET

Fig. 10   Milk Street, nos. 45 and 50.

NAISH'S STREET (E SIDE)
developed c.1690–1705

No. 38, a shop, originally a dwelling of A1 plan, with two storeys and an attic. The sash windows in the elevation to York Street, each of eighteen lights with thick glazing bars, are original. The interior has been extensively altered, so that the stack and winder-stairs have been removed. The axial ceiling-beams are chamfered with stepped plain stops.

No. 39, of A2 plan, with a cellar, two storeys and an attic, built on a plot 29ft long and abutted by nos. 38 and 40. Blocked earlier windows are visible in the rear elevation, where one has a stone frame, with hood-mould. The cellar has a stone segmented barrel-vault. A cross-passage divides the ground floor into a hall and parlour; but whether this is the original arrangement is uncertain, since the chamfered axial ceiling-beam has stepped plain stops at the stack and S gable ends only. The partition on the S (now removed) is probably on the line of the partition between the hall and parlour. The door to the garden is original. The winder-stair is against the stack on the street side, formerly lit by small windows, now blocked, below the first and attic floors. The roof is of butt-purlin construction, two open trusses with cambered collars dividing it into three bays.

Pl. 9

No. 40, c.1693, of A1 or A3 plan, originally with two storeys and an attic, the front cell probably similar in plan to no. 43, and occupying a plot 18ft wide. Not examined internally.

No. 41, of A4 plan, originally with two storeys and an attic. The roof has been raised, probably in the late 19th century, and a blocked gable window is visible in the front elevation. The dwelling was built between nos. 40 and 42, occupying a plot 18½ft wide. The ground-floor plan is possibly original, consisting of a parlour, hall and winder-stairs, the stairs lying between the parlour and an outshut at the rear. The axial ceiling-beam is cased.

Pl. 16

No. 42, of A3 plan, originally with two storeys and an attic, occupying a plot 17ft wide. The front cell, once similar in plan to no. 43, was much altered in the 19th century, when the stack and axial ceiling-beams were removed and the attic floor raised to a full storey.

Pl. 16

No. 43, of A3 plan with two storeys and an attic,

abutting no. 42 and occupying a plot 19ft wide. The street elevation has two original first-floor windows with hood-moulds and recessed hollow-chamfered mullions and has been built up over an attic gable. The front cell consists of a hall, originally probably entered from the street, with a cross-passage being inserted later. The axial ceiling-beam is chamfered with stepped plain stops; there are moulded risers to the winder-stairs which are against the stack in the S gable wall. The gabled cross-wing has a cellar under, was formerly unheated, and is probably a contemporary or near-contemporary addition to the front cell.

No. 46 (W part), of A1 plan with two storeys and a gabled attic, abutting no. 43 and occupying a plot 20ft wide. The ground floor consists of the hall with one room above on the first and attic floors. The winder-stair and stack are against the S end-wall, the axial ceiling-beams to the ground and first floors are chamfered. The roof is carried on rough-hewn purlins between the gable walls.

No. 46 (E part), of A1 plan with one storey and an attic, abutting the W part of no. 46. The axial ceiling-beam is chamfered with a runout stop at the stack end. The winder-stair has been removed.

Nos. 52–53, before 1745, pair of dwellings, two storeys, each of A1 plan subdivided at ground-floor level to contain a living-room, service lobby and stairs. The first floors are each divided into two rooms, the plank-and-muntin partition in no. 53 being original (and the only example recorded in the survey area). No. 53 abuts no. 54.

Nos. 54–55, before 1745, leased by a broadweaver in 1745–56. A pair of dwellings, each of two storeys, possibly built as one house of A3 plan, with a weaving shop. The original stack is in the SW end-wall with the central stack possibly being a later insertion. There is a partly-blocked wide louvred window-opening to the SW ground-floor room and wide casement windows at first-floor level. The five cross beams are plastered; there are several reset plain panelled pine partitions. The roof of no. 54 has possibly been raised.

No. 56, of A1 or A3 plan with two storeys and an attic, abutting no. 50 and occupying a plot 17½ft wide. The axial ceiling-beam spans the hall and the alley leading to no. 52–55, showing that the construction of the latter was an afterthought. The stack in the S end-wall

ELEVATION

GROUND FLOOR PLAN

post 1813 additions omitted

blocked three-light window

stack removed

cellar below

HALL   PARLOUR

38   39

gable

stairs removed

HALL

original stack removed

HALL   HALL   HALL

41   42   43   46

REAR ELEVATION No. 39

DETAIL No. 39

(a)

6 0   6   12 inches

5 0 10 20 30 cms.

GROUND FLOOR PLAN

52 53

54

55

NAISH'S STREET
EAST SIDE

10   0   10   20   30   40   50 feet

5   0   5   10   15 metres

plank and muntin partition - first floor No. 53, facing south

Fig. 11   Naish's Street, E side. Nos. 38–43, 46 and 52–55.

has been rebuilt. At first-floor level, there is a blocked window to the street elevation. The date of the lean-to addition at the rear is uncertain.

No. 57, of A1 or A3 plan, with two storeys and an attic, probably abutting no. 56 and occupying a plot 17½ft wide. The axial ceiling-beam is cased, and the doorframe to the rear extension is ovolo-moulded with stepped plain stops and an original door. The cross

ceiling-beam at first floor is chamfered with stepped plain stops and is the base of an open truss which has been repositioned after the roof was raised. The date of the outshut is uncertain.

No. 58, originally of A1 or A3 plan, with two storeys and an attic, possibly rebuilt in the 19th century; no early features remain internally.

GROUND FLOOR PLAN

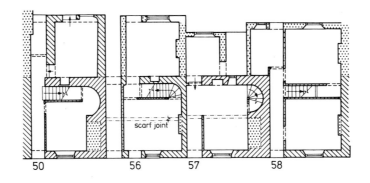

50   56   57   58

ELEVATION

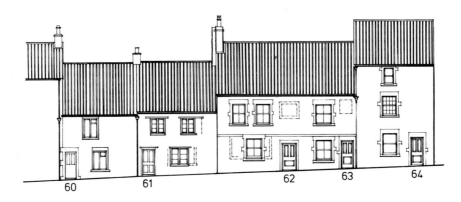

60   61   62   63   64

GROUND FLOOR PLAN

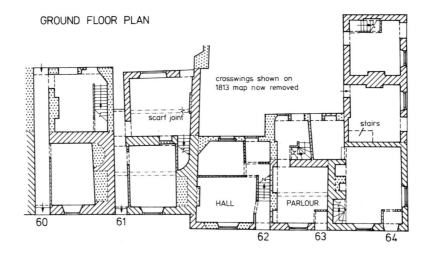

60   61   62   63   64

NAISH'S STREET
EAST SIDE

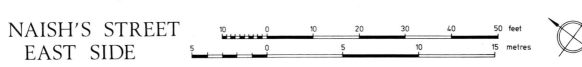

Fig. 12   Naish's Street, E side. Nos. 50, 56–58 and 60–64.

Nos. 60 and 61, pair of dwellings, each of two storeys. The infill of parts of earlier windows is visible in the street elevation. Only no. 61, which abuts no. 60, was examined internally; as built, it was probably of A1 or A3 plan. The axial ceiling-beam is cased. The rear gabled wing has a blocked window and is unheated.

Nos. 62 and 63, formerly The Dolphin Inn, originally one dwelling of two storeys, between and abutting nos. 61 and 64. The part blocking of earlier windows and the original stack in the N end-wall are visible in the street elevation. Internally, the building has been much altered in the 19th century, and parts of the original E wall have been demolished. In no. 63, the cased axial ceiling-beam remains. The original plan, indicated on the 1813 map, was possibly of class B4, L-shaped with a hall and unheated parlour separated by a cross-passage, with two separate cross-wings to the rear, the smaller containing a winder-stair. The relationship between nos. 62/63 and 64 is not absolutely clear.

Pl. 1

Pl. 16

No. 64, of A1 plan with two storeys and an attic, consisting originally of one cell, built against no. 63 and occupying a plot 17ft wide. The stack in the N end-wall has been much altered; internally, there are no axial ceiling-beams and all joinery is of the 19th century. Immediately to the NE are nos. 1 and 2 Baker Street; houses of A1 plan, of early 18th-century date, with the stairs opposite the stack.

NAISH'S STREET (W SIDE)
developed c.1690–1706

. 13, 14
18

Nos. 4 and 5, built c.1692, originally one house, of A4 plan, with two storeys and an attic. There are three main cells, the outshut being a later addition to the original L-shaped plan. The principal range facing the street contains the parlour and hall, entered from a cross-passage, a later addition, which also gives access to the unheated rear-wing which may be original. The axial ceiling-beams, chamfered with stepped plain stops, are tenoned into a cross beam; the hall gives access to the winder-stairs which are against the stack. The newel and risers are moulded and the doors to the stairs and the cupboard below have raised fielded panels of similar pattern. The roofs to the principal range and cross-wing are of butt-purlin construction.

Pl. 12

No. 10, built 1693 by Samuel Whitchurch, cardmaker. Dwelling built against no. 9 (demolished), originally of A1 plan, with two storeys and an attic. The interior

has been considerable altered in the 19th century. On the ground floor, the fireplace opening and the winder-stair, which survives above the first floor, are now blocked and the axial ceiling-beam is cased. The cellar has a stone barrel-vault and was originally accessible from outside the house at the rear. The rear cell is an outshut containing a heated parlour, of before 1813 and probably contemporary with a diamond-patterned tiled pavement in the passage beside the front and rear rooms; two additions with lean-to roofs are of similar date, one having a window with a sliding and a fixed sash.

Pl. 7

Nos. 11–14, originally each of two storeys and an attic, the front cells of both being almost identical in construction and detail. The stairs have moulded risers, and where visible the ceiling-beams are chamfered with stepped plain stops. Nos. 11 and 12 were of A1 plan; nos. 13 and 14 were of A3 plan. All were remodelled in the late 19th century at much the same time, each now having identical door and window reveals, marginal glazing and similar rainwater heads.

In no. 11, the door to the stairs on the first floor is probably original. The rear cell, an outshut, is an addition of before 1813. In the NW corner was possibly a furnace, now mainly demolished at ground-floor level, but with the flue converted into a cupboard on the first floor.

In no. 12, the partition between the hall and passage is probably of the 19th century. The grate to the first-floor front room, contained by four horizontal bars, is original. The roof is carried on two rough-hewn purlins between the gable walls. The rear cell is an outshut of before 1813.

In no. 13, the rear cell is possibly contemporary. It is of one storey and an attic and was originally unheated and has a gabled roof; the axial ceiling-beam to the ground floor corresponds to the former position of the S wall as shown on the 1813 map and confirmed by the exterior profile of the gable.

Pl. 1

In no. 14, the rear cell is of two storeys, was originally unheated and has a gabled roof. The dwelling was much altered in the 19th century, when the winder-stairs and stack were removed at ground-floor level.

Pl. 7

Nos. 15–16, early 18th century, pair of dwellings, each of A1 plan, with two storeys and an attic, built in the rear parts of the plots occupied on the street frontage by nos. 13 and 14, and approached by the alley-way between nos. 14 and 18. Internally,. the houses were much altered in the 19th century, when additional rooms, now ruinous, were added on the NW side.

NAISH'S STREET
WEST SIDE

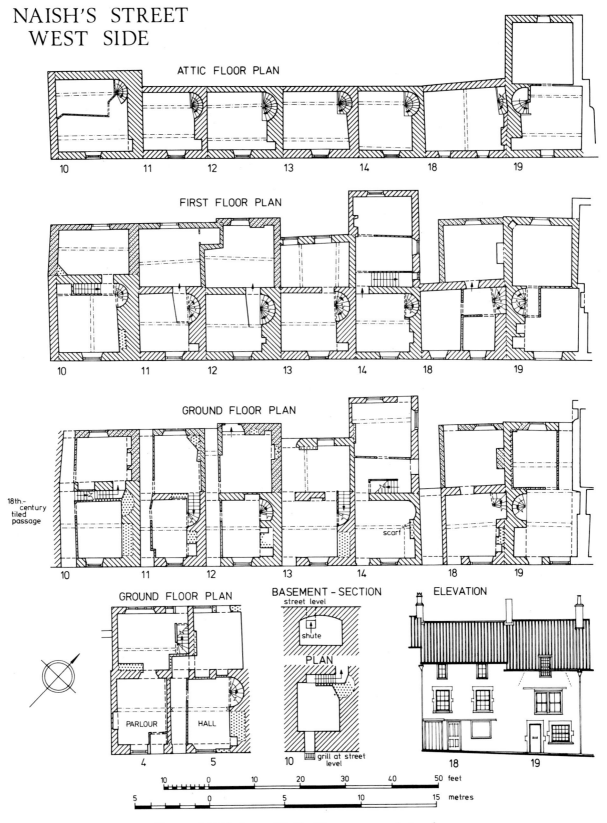

Fig. 13   Naish's Street, W side. Nos. 4, 5, 10–14, 18 and 19.

No. 18, built between nos. 14 and 19, originally of A1 plan, with two storeys and an attic. The chimney-piece to the first-floor room is possibly original. The rear cell is an outshut, added before 1813.

No. 19, of A3 plan with two storeys, a cellar and an attic. There is no internal wall between the two cells, the first floor being supported on three axial beams, all cased. The N wall was partly or completely demolished when no. 20 was totally rebuilt in the 19th century. The line of a former attic gable is visible in the street elevation. The front cell consists of the hall with one room on each of the two floors above; there is a winder-stair against the stack on the S end-wall. The front roof is carried on rough-hewn purlins between the end walls. The rear cell was originally unheated, but was much altered in the early 18th century when the window opening was partly blocked and the walls lined with panelling, raised and fielded in two heights, with matching doors and a corner cupboard, all of which have now been removed. The cellar is accessible only from no. 20. The former width of the partly blocked first-floor rear window indicates that the room was used as a workshop. The gabled roof is of butt-purlin construction with one open and one closed truss.

No. 23, of A3 plan with two storeys and an attic. It abuts no. 22 and occupies a plot 17ft wide. The front cell originally consisted of one heated room on each floor with the winder-stair against the stack in the N end-wall. The axial ceiling-beam to the ground floor and the doorframe between the front and rear cells are chamfered with ogee(?) stops. The rear cell was originally unheated; the axial ceiling-beam to the ground floor is chamfered and stopped. The gabled roof is of butt-purlin construction with one closed truss.

Nos. 24 and 25, originally one house, of A4 plan, consisting of three main cells. It abuts no. 23 and occupies a plot about 24ft wide. The attic windows are in gables on the street side. The house was divided into two separate dwellings in the 18th century, when an additional staircase and partitions were inserted. Owing to these and later alterations, it is uncertain whether the front cell, with the winder-stair against the stack, contained at ground level one large hall or whether there was also a parlour. Above, there are two rooms on the first and attic floors, the roof being of butt-purlin construction with one closed truss. Both the gabled cross-wings to the rear were originally heated and are

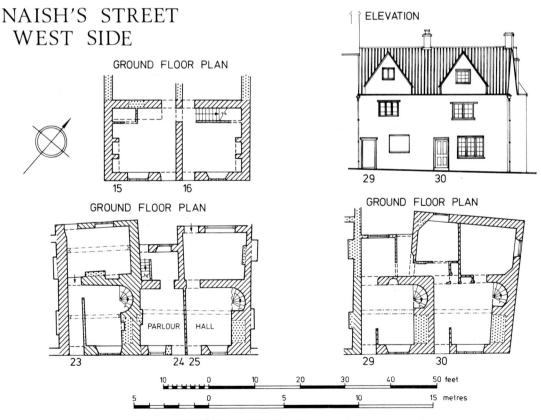

NAISH'S STREET WEST SIDE

GROUND FLOOR PLAN

15   16

GROUND FLOOR PLAN

PARLOUR   HALL

23   24 25

ELEVATION

29   30

GROUND FLOOR PLAN

29   30

10   0   10   20   30   40   50 feet

5   0   5   10   15 metres

Fig. 14   Naish's Street, W side. Nos. 15, 16, 23–25, 29 and 30.

probably contemporary with or close in date to the front cell. Parts of no. 24 were inaccessible.

Nos. 29 and 30, c.1705, pair of dwellings of A1 and A3 plan respectively, with two storeys and an attic, occupying together a plot 32ft wide. In both, the front cell consists of a hall with an axial ceiling-beam and with the winder-stair against the stack in the N end-wall. The gabled cross-wing to the rear of no. 30 is probably contemporary and was unheated. In 1975 there were several original cupboard doors in the ground-floor rooms of no. 30. The rear first-floor window to no. 29 has chamfered stone mullions and a hood-mould. On Pl. 4 the street side, the attic windows are in gables.

SELWOOD ROAD (E SIDE) 1690s

Fig. 15, Pl. 19

Nos. 73 and 74, pair of dwellings, of two storeys and each of A3 plan, with two cells together occupying a plot 33½ft wide. The front cell consisted of one room on each floor with the winder-stair against the stack in the S end-wall. There are moulded risers to the stairs and the axial ceiling-beams to the ground floors are chamfered with ogee stops at the gable ends. In no. 73, the doorframe at the back of the passage is ovolo-moulded with stops. The roofs are carried on rough-hewn purlins between the gable walls. The rear cells are one storey outshuts, originally unheated and occupying only part of the plot width. Both are possibly contemporary with the front parts; in neither are there indications of earlier windows, now blocked, such as would have existed if the front cells had been built to stand alone. In no. 73 a small cellar has been Pls. 9, 11 inserted.

Nos. 85 and 86, originally one house of A4 plan, abutting no. 84 and abutted by no. 87, of two storeys and an attic, occupying a plot 33½ft wide. The front cell consisted originally of an unheated parlour and the hall which was entered from the street and has a winder-stair with moulded risers against the stack in the S end-wall; the axial ceiling-beam, partly cased, is chamfered with stepped plain stops at the stack end. The attic windows were in gables on the street side; the roof is of butt-purlin construction with one closed truss dividing the attic floor into two rooms. Only the southernmost of the three gabled cross-wings is possibly original, for the other two both partly conceal a blocked ovolo-moulded wooden window in the rear elevation to the principal range.

No. 87, of A2 plan, consisting of two storeys, abutting no. 86 and occupying a plot 24ft wide. The single ground-floor room is entered from the street; the axial ceiling-beam is chamfered with stepped plain stops. The oak winder-stair is against the stack on the street side, as with no. 78.

SELWOOD ROAD (W SIDE)
1680s or early 1690s

Fig. 15

No. 14, of A1 plan, with two storeys and an attic. The plan consists of one room on each floor with the winder-stair against the stack in the W end-wall. The axial ceiling-beam to the ground floor is cased.

No. 19, of B4 plan. Originally with one storey and an attic, now of two storeys. The principal range contains an unheated parlour and the hall, the latter entered from the street and with the stack, now blocked, in the S end-wall. The position of the original partition between the rooms is indicated by stepped plain stops to the chamfered axial ceiling-beams. Two cross-wings contain the stairs and an unheated room. The latter, although structurally an addition, may nevertheless be part of the original plan. If it had been added later, the original back wall would probably have been retained between the two rooms. The interior was considerably altered in the 19th century, when the winder-stair was replaced and the first floor to the front and the rear wing was raised. Part of the E wall has been rebuilt. Three original stone mullioned windows survive.

Pls. 10,

No. 20, originally of A2 plan, with two storeys and an attic, occupying a plot 24ft wide. It was much altered in the 19th century, so that the original plan cannot be fully discerned. The stairs were against the stack in the W end-wall; inserted in their place are two cupboards possibly removed from elsewhere in the house; one is recessed with shaped shelves. The sophisticated bolection-moulded chimneypiece is of the late 17th century and may be in situ. Against the stack on the first floor is a cupboard with decoration in Jacobean style, probably of the 18th century. The roof is of butt-purlin construction.

Pls. 12,

Nos. 21 and 22, originally one house with two storeys and an attic, occupying a plot 30ft wide and built to a B2 plan. The front elevation and the interior were completely rebuilt in the 19th century. The only original features remaining are the curved recess for

31

SELWOOD ROAD. EAST SIDE

SELWOOD ROAD. WEST SIDE

YORK STREET

YORK STREET &
SELWOOD ROAD
WEST SIDE

not surveyed
PARLOUR   HALL

HALL   HALL
73   74

85 86   87

HALL
14

HALL   PARLOUR
19

HALL
20

PARLOUR

PARLOUR
21
22   stairs removed

HALL

PARLOUR   HALL
23

2 3

6

18
HALL

PARLOUR

PARLOUR   gable

open

YORK STREET

HALL   HALL PARLOUR   HALL

line of original partition
29   30   31
SELWOOD ROAD

10   0   10   20   30   40   50 feet
5   0   5   10   15 metres

Fig. 15   Selwood Road and York Street. Selwood Road: E side, nos. 73, 74, and 85–87; W side, nos. 14, 19–23, and 29–31. York Street, nos. 2, 3, 6 and 18.

the winder-stair and the blocked stack in the E end-wall.

Pl. 5

No. 23, late 17th century, of A2 plan, with two storeys and a cellar, abutting no. 22. The division of the ground floor into two rooms is possibly original, providing an unheated parlour and a hall with the winder-stair against the stack in the N end-wall. The axial ceiling-beam is cased.

No. 29, before 1688, of A3 plan, with two storeys and an attic, and abutting no. 30. The front cell has one room on each floor with the winder-stair against the stack in the S end-wall. The axial ceiling-beams are cased. The rear wing is unheated; a now blocked door led to no. 18 York Street.

No. 30, before 1688, of A4 plan, with two storeys and an attic, and abutted by nos. 29 and 31. The ground-floor window has a hood-mould over. Entrance was probably into the hall, originally partitioned, or into one large room. The axial ceiling-beam is chamfered with stepped plain stops at the stack and N gable-ends. There are moulded risers to the winder-stair, which is against the stack in the S end-wall. An unheated cross-wing is contemporary, but has been rebuilt above the first floor so that it now partly abuts no. 18 York Street. On the first floor there is a 17th-century oak door with six panels in three heights, separating the two principal rooms. A door to the rear cross-wing is possibly of the same date, being similar to a door with two ovolo-moulded panels separating the two rooms of the principal range at attic level. The roof is of butt-purlin construction with one closed and one open truss, sub-dividing it into three bays.

Pl. 10

No. 31, before 1688, of A3 plan with two storeys and an attic, abutting no. 30. The rear cell is of one room and is possibly original. The front cell contains one room on each floor with a winder-stair against the stack in the N end-wall. On the ground floor is a 17th-century cupboard door, studded and with three panels in three heights. On the first floor there is an original lobby to the stairs with two oak doors each having four ovolo-moulded panels in two heights. The first-floor and attic windows to the N gable-wall and the street elevation have ovolo-moulded stone mullions with hood-moulds. The roof is carried on rough-hewn purlins between the gable walls.

Nos. 29, 30 and 31 occupy a plot 31ft by 60½ft, probably the plot in New Close referred to as already built upon

in 1688, and part of the same block as another plot developed in 1679.

TRINITY STREET (S SIDE)

No. 1, The King's Head Inn (excluding the E part which was formerly part of no. 2), c.1680. House of B5 plan with four main cells. The principal range 40¾ft long and 18½ft deep, is of two storeys with a loft and one original chimney stack at the W end. The 1813 map indicates that between the two cross-wings was a further wing containing the stairs and a lobby providing entrance from the S. At attic level, a partition cut for a gable and the absence of the lower purlin provide further evidence for a cross-wing now removed. Entrance from Trinity Street is through a cross-passage leading on the W to the hall, the fireplace in the W wall having ovolo-moulded stone jambs and lintel and a brick fireback in herringbone bond. On the E is the parlour, one window of which is now blocked. The axial ceiling-beam is chamfered with stepped plain stops in the hall and at the E end in the parlour. The existing windows to the ground floor are renewed; the first floor and loft have chamfered renewed window cases with hood-moulds. Two attic gables to the street elevation are shown on a photograph of c.1925. The original plan of the first floor is not discernible; beside the chimneystack a door with six panels in two heights is of an original cupboard. One doorframe is ovolo-moulded with ogee stops. The roof is of butt-purlin construction and is subdivided into four bays by three open trusses. The projecting wing to the W is of two storeys, unheated and with walls of identical thickness to the main range. The added wing to the E was possibly a kitchen or brewhouses with a chimneystack in the S gable-end and was of one storey with a loft. An original timber window with diamond-shaped mullions remains on the ground floor. The walls are slightly thinner than those of the other two ranges and were probably raised and refenestrated in the 19th century. Internally, all three surviving ranges are very much altered.

Pls. 3, 12

No. 2 (including W part of No. 1), c.1680, of B4 plan. The main range, occupying a plot 30½ft long and 18½ft deep, is of two storeys and an attic, and was built against no. 1. Three of the windows to the front elevation are original and had ovolo-moulded stone mullions with hood-moulds. The entrance from the street is into a cross-passage. To the E was probably the parlour; to the W is the hall having access to the

GROUND FLOOR PLAN

GROUND FLOOR PLAN

ATTIC FLOOR PLAN

GROUND FLOOR PLAN

HOUSE AT
REAR OF
NO. 11

GROUND FLOOR PLAN

ELEVATION

TRINITY STREET
SOUTH SIDE

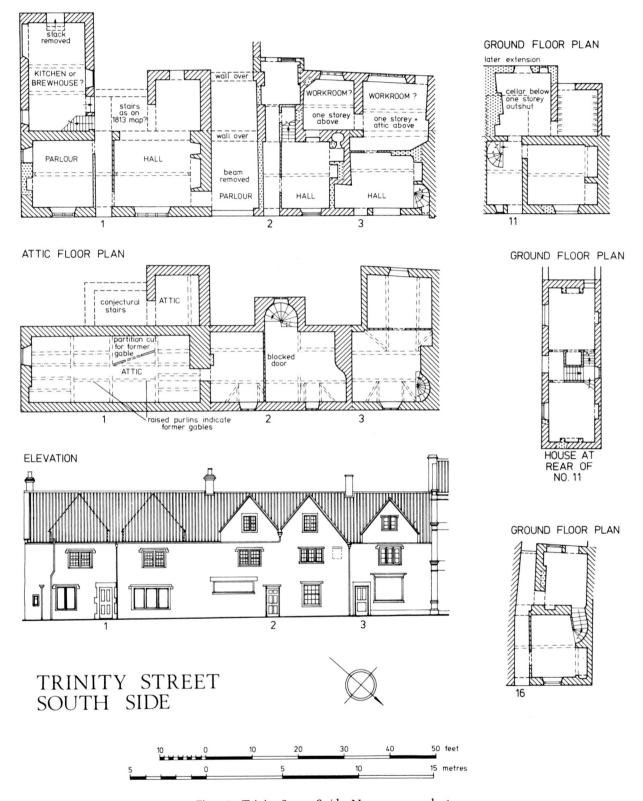

Fig. 16   Trinity Street, S side. Nos. 1-3, 11 and 16.

stairs and heated by a stack in the W gable wall, now partly blocked. A niche to the N of the stack has been removed so as to enlarge no. 3; in the S wall is a cupboard with six raised fielded panels in two heights. The axial ceiling-beam is cased. To the S, the later cross-passage provided access under the stairs to the kitchen through a repositioned doorframe, ovolo-moulded with plain stops. The E projecting wing, unheated and of two storeys, is partly demolished at ground-floor level and the original arrangements cannot be discerned. The stairs have been repositioned to provide access to a later rear addition, but retain some of the original moulded oak risers. The first and attic floors of the main range each consisted of two chambers. The N room on the first floor has a stone fireplace with a fluted keystone to an ogee arch, it may be original but is more likely to be of the early 18th century. The blocked doorframe between the attic rooms is chamfered with plain stops. The roof is of butt-purlin construction and is subdivided into three bays by one open and one closed truss.

Pls. 3, 14

No. 3, c.1680, of A3 plan, with two storeys and an attic. The first and attic-floor windows to the street elevation and the ground and first-floor windows at the rear are original, having ovolo-moulded stone mullions with hood-moulds. The N part is of two storeys and an attic, and was built against no. 2, occupying a plot about 18ft long and 18½ft deep. The hall which was entered from the street, and heated by a now partly blocked stack in the W gable-wall, provides access to the oak winder-stair which has a blocked window to the street. The axial ceiling-beams to the ground and first floor are cased. The S part consists of two rooms built against and abutted by original parts of no. 2, showing that the houses were constructed at the same time. The E part is of two storeys and was formerly part of no. 2. The fireplace on the ground floor is of late 18th-century date. The W part is unheated, and has two storeys with an attic. The roof to the N range is carried on cut purlins between the gable walls; the roofs over the S rooms are of similar date.

Pls. 3, 14

No. 7, c.1680, of B4 plan consisting of three main storeys, a cellar, attics and lofts. The exterior is rendered and the fenestration is entirely of the 19th century. The cellar below the S wing has brick barrel-vaults, a central brick pillar with freestone base and capital, vents or shutes and a stone sink below the stairs, the lowest of which is stone. At ground floor level the main range occupies a plot 28ft long and 18½ft deep and originally probably consisted of an unheated parlour and a hall with the stack in the W end-wall. The

axial ceiling-beam is chamfered with stepped plain stops. Entrance to both rooms was probably from the stairs lobby, where the doorframe of the entrance from the S is ovolo-moulded with ogee stops and has an original door and glazed fanlight. In the hall a ventilated cupboard on the N side of the stack is original. The fireplaces in both the hall and the rear S, or kitchen, wing have oak bressumers with ashlar jambs. A blocked entrance between the kitchen and no. 6 indicates that it may have been shared by two houses.

The stairs to the first and attic floors have closed strings, moulded risers, turned balusters with ball finials on the newels and a moulded handrail. Doorframes to the first and attic-floor rooms are ovolo-moulded or chamfered with ogee or stepped runout stops respectively. On the attic landing is an ashlar-lined niche, possibly for a light. A winder-stair with moulded risers provides access to a loft over the S wing and was probably added. A loft over the N wing, lit by windows with wooden shutters in each gable wall, was accessible only by ladder. The roofs are of butt-purlin construction, the principal open truss over the S wing having an arched collar.

Pls. 6, 8

Nos. 8–22. Part of the Katherine Close development, c.1718–22.

No. 11, formerly The Trooper Inn. House of A4 plan with four main cells. Four of the windows to the street elevation are original, some with ovolo-mouldings, some with rectangular-section mullions with a recessed chamfer. The principal range, 26ft long and 17ft deep, is built against no. 10 and consists of two storeys and an attic. The entrance lobby contains the stairs which survive as a winder-stair above the first floor and as a stone stair providing access to the original cellar, now under a later outshut. The hall, entered from the lobby, has a stack in the W gable-wall with an oak bressumer over the fireplace. The axial ceiling-beams to the hall and lobby are chamfered and cased. The outshut was possibly built as a kitchen with a stack in the E wall. A smaller room to the W is of uncertain function, but is possibly original, having a framed first floor and gabled roof over. At first-floor level, a cupboard against the stack may be original, the door being ovolo-moulded with one raised fielded panel. At roof level, the purlins run between the gable walls with one closed truss dividing the cell containing the hall into two bays.

Pl. 4

House behind no. 11, of two storeys, constructed before 1813. The plan now consists of a central staircase with a heated room to either side; a blocked window behind the stack on the NE side shows that originally

35

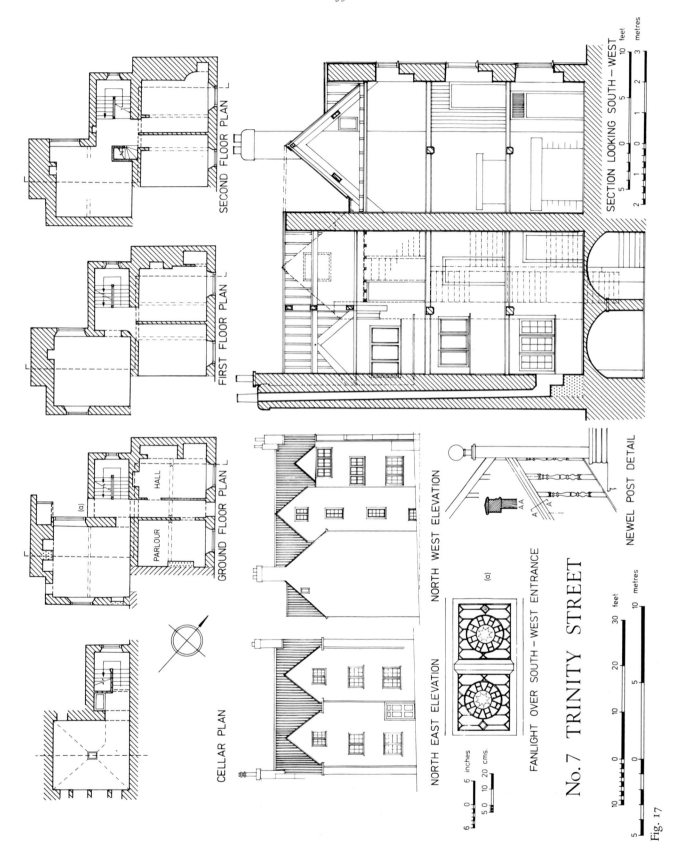

SECOND FLOOR PLAN

FIRST FLOOR PLAN

GROUND FLOOR PLAN

HALL

PARLOUR

(a)

CELLAR PLAN

SECTION LOOKING SOUTH—WEST

feet
metres

NEWEL POST DETAIL

A A

NORTH WEST ELEVATION

(a)

FANLIGHT OVER SOUTH—WEST ENTRANCE

NORTH EAST ELEVATION

No. 7 TRINITY STREET

Fig. 17

6 inches
10 20 cms.
5 0

30 feet
20
10 metres
10
5
0
0

10
5

a different plan may have been intended. In each of the ground-floor rooms are cupboard doors of the early 18th century, with raised fielded panels and strap-hinges. Other internal features are predominantly of the late 18th or early 19th centuries and include the stairs which have a moulded pine handrail of thin section with balusters of square section. The present plan is possibly of the same date.

Pl. 13 No. 16, of A3 plan, with two storeys and an attic. On the ground floor, the original fireplace has ashlar reveals, an inglenook seat and a rough-hewn oak bressumer. The axial ceiling-beam is of elm, and is chamfered with stepped plain stops.

Fig. 18
VALLIS WAY (N SIDE)
New Close, developed by the 1680s, possibly from the mid 17th century.

No. 31, The Globe. Inn of B2 or B4 plan with two storeys and an attic, occupying a plot 31ft wide. Internally, it has been much altered in the 19th and 20th centuries and only the parts illustrated could be examined. The stack, now blocked, is in the E gable-wall; the axial ceiling-beam is cased. There was probably a staircase wing to the rear, now removed.

No. 32, now a shop. House of A2 plan with two storeys and an attic, occupying a plot 35ft wide and abutting no. 31. Originally it consisted of one range containing an unheated parlour and a hall with the stack in the E end-wall. The stack has been removed, but at attic level the recess for the winder-stair against it is still visible. The existing cross-passage walls are of brick and are a later insertion. The roof is of butt-purlin construction with two open trusses. Parts of blocked earlier windows are visible on the street side. Pl. 2

No. 33, now a shop. House, originally perhaps of A4 plan with two storeys, occupying a plot 22ft wide and built between no. 32 and a house to the E since demolished. The ground floor has been much altered, but the original plan may be discerned. The front cell possibly contained two rooms with a winder-stair against the stack in the W end-wall, the floor above being carried on two cross beams, as at no. 18 York Street, now cased. The cross beam on the SE side possibly corresponded to the division between hall and parlour. The wing to the rear could not be examined in detail. The stack visible in the E end-wall belonged to the dwelling to the E, the original W stack to no. 33 still being visible at roof level. Pl. 2

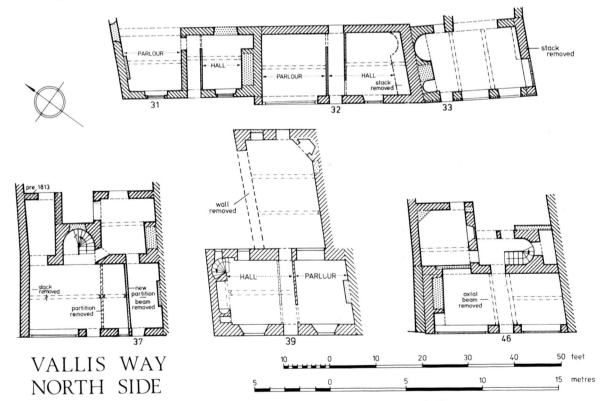

VALLIS WAY
NORTH SIDE

Fig. 18   Vallis Way, N side. Nos. 31–33, 37, 39 and 46.

No. 37, of B4 plan with two storeys, consisting originally of three main cells, and abutting no. 38. Part of the principal range is now used as a shop. Originally there was a hall, entered from the street, and a parlour, the position of the partition between the two being shown by ogee stops to the chamfered ceiling-beams; a scarfed joint indicates the former stack position. Two cross-wings to the rear are contemporary, the first contains the winder-stair with a moulded newel and moulded risers. In the second, the axial ceiling-beam is supported by the stack which is original. The doorframe to the stairs is chamfered with ogee stops. A small unheated room to the W of the stairs is of uncertain date, but is certainly before 1813.

No. 39, of A4 plan with two storeys and an attic; it occupies a plot 32ft wide and abuts no. 40. The principal range fronting the street consisted of an unheated parlour and the hall, entrance being into the latter. The axial ceiling-beam, which remains only in the hall, is chamfered with ogee stops. When the blocked up fireplace was re-opened and the oak bressumer exposed, two triangular datestones were found, the one inscribed with the figures '16', and the other inscribed with unidentifiable figures. The winder-stairs, against the stack, have moulded risers and are lit by a window with an ovolo-moulded frame and original glazing. The roof is of butt-purlin construction with three open trusses dividing the attic room into four bays. The rear wall is built up to form a gable to the rear wing and the absence of a lower purlin from the main roof at this point demonstrates that the two ranges are contemporary.

The rear wing has been much altered. On the ground and first floors, the cross beams are chamfered with stepped plain stops; the fireplace in the NE corner is probably a later insertion. The roof is of butt-purlin construction.

No. 46, now a shop. House of B4 plan with two storeys and an attic, occupying a plot 30½ft wide and abutting no. 47. Entrance to the principal range was probably into the hall, giving access to the stairs and an unheated parlour. The ceiling beams are cased. On the first floor, one axial beam is chamfered with stepped plain stops; a cupboard against the stack is original. The roof is of butt-purlin construction, two closed trusses dividing the attic bay into three bays.

To the rear are two cross-wings, both contemporary with the main range. One contains the stairs, of late 18th-century date, with closed strings, square-sectioned balusters and a moulded mahogany handrail, but

probably in the same position as an earlier winder-stair. A second originally unheated wing is of one storey and an attic, with a gabled roof of butt-purlin construction.

VALLIS WAY (S SIDE) Fig. 19, Pl. 3

No. 4, before 1697, originally of B5 plan with two storeys, an attic and a cellar, occupying a plot 50ft wide. The principal range is entered from the street by a cross-passage giving access to a parlour and hall, both heated, and to the stairs. The ground and first floors were considerably altered in the 19th century when the street side was refenestrated, the rooms refurbished with new joinery and plasterwork and the axial ceiling-beams encased. At attic level there are two original doors of oak with three panels in three heights. The central cross-wing to the rear contains the stairs; to the first floor they are 19th century in date, having cut strings with a moulded mahogany handrail. Above the first floor the oak newel, treads and risers may be original, having closed strings, slender turned balusters and a moulded pine handrail.

The gabled cross-wings to either side of the stairs are also probably original. The SE wing has a cased axial ceiling-beam.

No. 5, 1697, of A4 plan with two storeys and an attic, occupying a plot 29ft wide and abutting no. 4. It was built as one house but later divided so that the SE half is now part of no. 4. There was a regular design to the street elevation. At ground-floor level, the blockings of earlier windows are visible. At first-floor level there are windows with ovolo-moulded stone mullions and transoms, and a datestone reading 'Time trieth troth IVNE y^{e}3 JS 1697'. An oval segmented stone window to the stairwell has original glazing.

Entrance was probably into the hall, giving access to an unheated parlour. The cross-wing to the rear is of two storeys, originally unheated, and abuts no. 4. Pl. 16

Nos. 6 and 7, originally one house, of A4 plan with two storeys and an attic. Entrance was formerly into the hall, giving access to an unheated parlour.

The original doorframe to the parlour survives and is ovolo-moulded with ogee stops; the axial ceiling-beams are chamfered with stepped plain stops. There are moulded risers to the stairs, which are against the stack and were formerly lit by two windows, both now blocked. The first floor possibly contained three rooms; the roof is of butt-purlin construction, subdividing the attic floor into three bays. On the SW side, the purlin

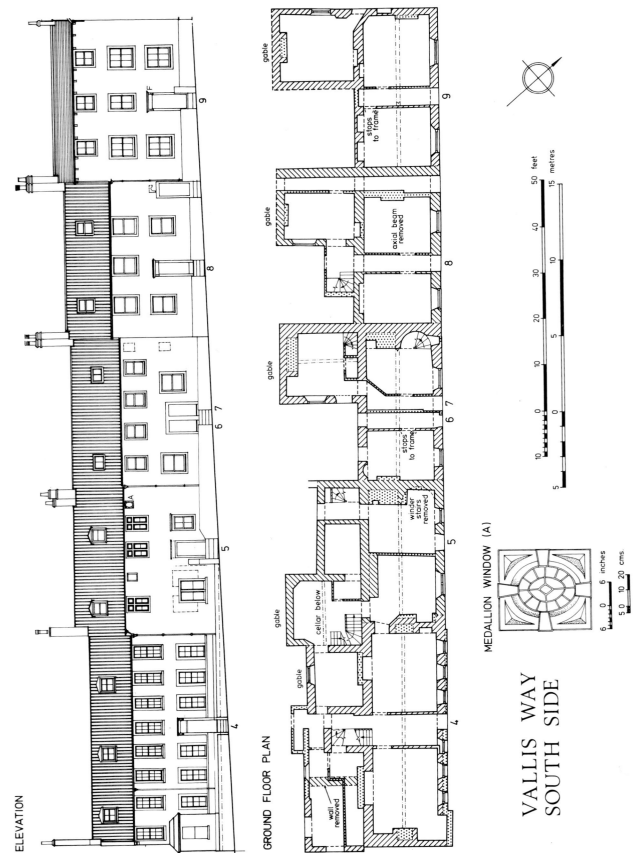

ELEVATION

GROUND FLOOR PLAN

gable gable gable gable gable gable

stops to frame

axial beam removed

winder stairs removed

stops to frame

cellar below

wall removed

MEDALLION WINDOW (A)

VALLIS WAY
SOUTH SIDE

Fig. 19 Vallis Way, S side. Nos. 4–9.

adjacent to the rear cross wing is raised above the level of the other purlins, as at no. 3 Castle Street and no. 39 Vallis Way, indicating that the front and rear ranges are contemporary.

The rear cell is of two storeys and has an original stack in the S end-wall; at ground-floor level, the axial ceiling-beam is chamfered; the doorframes linking the ground and first-floor rooms to the front range are ovolo-moulded with nicked ogee stops.

The street elevation retains the original fenestration, similar to no. 5 except that the mullions and transoms have been removed to allow the insertion of sash windows. One blocked window at the rear is of similar type.

Pl. 11

No. 8, of A4 plan with two storeys and an attic, originally of similar plan to nos. 5 and 6–7, but with an unheated cross-wing. The building was refenestrated and much altered internally in the 19th century, the winder-stairs and stack being removed to provide a passage to no. 8A. A blocked oval segmented window to the stairwell, similar to that of no. 5, is visible above the passage door. The roof is of similar construction to nos. 6–7, the tie-beams of the trusses forming ceiling joists chamfered with stepped plain stops.

No. 9, of A4 plan with two storeys and an attic; formerly similar to nos. 6 and 7. The building is partly ruinous and only the ground floor was surveyed. Entrance was originally into the hall. As at no. 5, there remains an original doorframe in the partition between the hall and the parlour, ovolo-moulded with nicked ogee stops. The axial ceiling-beam is chamfered with stepped plain stops at this partition and at each end. A

rear window with ovolo-moulded stone mullions and transoms is visible at first-floor level.

YORK STREET (N SIDE)

Fig. 15
Pl. 18

No. 18, late 17th century, of A2 plan with two storeys and an attic, occupying a plot 24ft wide and 60ft long and abutting no. 29 Selwood Road. The ground floor has been altered so that one room, probably an unheated parlour, is now a garage. Entrance from the street is to the hall with a winder-stair against the stack in the W end-wall. The cross ceiling-beams are chamfered with stepped plain stops.

YORK STREET (S SIDE)

Fig. 15
Pl. 18

Nos. 2 and 3, 18th century, originally one dwelling of A2 or A4 plan with two storeys and an attic. The original plan probably comprised two principal rooms on each floor with a stack in each end-wall; the partly-framed stair against the stack in no. 3 may be original. There is a mansard roof to the front elevation. The SW cross-wing may also be original.

No. 6, 18th century, originally of A2 plan with two storeys and an attic. The ground floor probably comprised an unheated parlour and a hall, the partition between them having recently been removed. A winder-stair, now repositioned, is against the stack in the W end-wall. The axial ceiling-beams are squared or rough-hewn without chamfers or stops.

APPENDIX 1

MAIN CLASSES OF DOCUMENTS CONSULTED

In the Public Record Office
Court of Exchequer: modern deeds (E214).
Court of Chancery: Chancery proceedings (C 2, 3, 5–12); Chancery Masters' exhibits (C 103–111, C 113, 114);
 Chancery Entry books of decrees and orders (C 33); Inquisitions Post Mortem, series II (C 142).
Court of Wards: Inquisitions Post Mortem (Wards 7).
Prerogative Court of Canterbury: registered copies of wills (Prob. 11); inventories (Prob. 3, 4).

In the Somerset Record Office
All accumulated collections listed under *Frome* in the topographical card index, including maps, deeds, ratebooks,
correspondence and historical notes.

In the Wiltshire Record Office
All accumulated collections listed under *Frome* and *Yerbury* in the topographical and persons' indices.

At the offices of Mendip District Council, Wells
The deeds to all Council property in the Trinity area.

At the offices of Somerset County Council, Taunton
The deeds to Council-owned property in Castle Street, Milk Street and Vallis Way.

At the Church of St John, Frome
Church rate books.

(Deeds to privately-owned property)
At the offices of Daniel and Cruttwell, Frome.
At the home of Mr and Miss Knight, 10 Naish's Street, Frome.
At the offices of J. W. Singer & Sons Ltd, Frome.
In Frome Museum, various deeds (including a copy of the ledger book containing the deeds transcribed by the
late J. O. Lewis, the original of which is in the possession of *Mr N. F. Maggs, Frome*).

APPENDIX 2

IDENTIFICATION OF LEASES PRIOR TO 1813

Most of the pre-1813 leases consulted were stray leases no longer associated with a particular named or numbered property. The following identifications of location are based on the close name, invariably given, sometimes on a street name, on the plot dimensions, and on any correlation between the above, the leaseholder's name, the yearly rent and corresponding details in the survey of 1753 (Longleat MS, WMR Box 28). In the latter, the individual house entries are arranged in geographical sequence, commencing at the Manor House, and then passing along successive streets.

STREET	HOUSE NO.	DATE OF LEASE	COMMENTS	REFERENCE
Old Presbytery		14 May 1725	formerly Manor House of St Katherine's	SRO DD/SAS/36/2
Baker St.	2, 3, 4	18 Mar 1758		deeds of 10 Naish's St.
Broad St.	46	30 Sep 1729	house nos. are for	SRO DD/SAS/36/2
,,	W side	17 Nov 1720	Selwood Road	,, ,, ,,
,,	,,	12 Sep 1710	refers back to 1689	,, ,, ,,
,,	,,	18 May 1693		SRO DD/S/HY box 6
,,	56–57	30 Oct 1716	adjacent to 9–11 Milk St.	SRO DD/SAS/36/2
Castle St.	B	1 Sep 1707		SRO DD/SAS/36/2
,,	7–8	4 Jun 1695		SRO DD/SAS/36/1
,,	14	8 Sep 1730	probable identification refers back to 1720	SRO DD/SAS/36/2
,,	17	20 Oct 1761	refers back to 1718	Frome Museum
,,	23	10 Nov 1716		SRO DD/SAS/36/2
Duke St.	9	28 Jun 1788	refers back to 1724	Frome Museum
Dyers Close Lane	S side	26 Mar 1737	refers back to 1722	JOL 62
Milk St.	9–11	19 Nov 1696	refers back to 1687	SRO SS/SAS/36/1
,,	S side	21 Oct 1686	refers to earlier lease	SRO DD/SAS/36/1
,,	26–26c	7 Aug 1721	refers back to 1698	SRO DD/SAS/36/2
,,	47–50	28 Aug 1773		SRO DD/LW/81 deeds no. 4
The Mint	1	20 Apr 1719		JOL 55
,,	1	11 Jan 1731		JOL 60
,,	6	1 Jul 1743		JOL 18
,,	7	20 Apr 1719		JOL 56
,,	7	27 Oct 1763	refers back to 1750	JOL 45
,,	10	8 Sep 1720		JOL, lent by Walwin
,,	10	24 Apr 1765	refers back to 1733	JOL 52
,,	10	10 May 1766	refers back to 1765	MDC 426
,,	10	20 Mar 1792	refers back to 1766	,, ,,
,,	17	25 Mar 1797		JOL 21
,,	N side	15 Sep 1718		JOL 54
Naish's St.	6–8	6 Sep 1732	refers back to 1692	JOL, lent by Walwin
,,	,,	24 Oct 1765		JOL 51
,,	10	20 Sep 1693	also deeds to present day	deeds to 10 Naish's St.
,,	13–14	1810	includes details from earlier leases	MDC 462
,,	29–30	15 Nov 1705	also other deeds to 1749	Daniel & Crutwell, Frome
,,	39	20 May 1743	refers back to 1732	SRO DD/SAS/36/2
,,	40	18 Apr 1705	refers back to 1693	,, ,, ,,
,,	48	31 Oct 1767	refers back to 1743	Frome Museum
,,	53, 54	1 Oct 1760	refers back to 1745	MDC 535
,,	62–64	18 Mar 1758	refers back to 1721	deeds of 10 Naish's St.
Peter St.	4b	25 May 1743	refers back to 1735	JOL 17
,,	8	5 Jun 1735	refers back to 1722	JOL 61
,,	9	25 Aug 1752	refers back to 1738	MDC 60
,,	10–12	2 Jan 1808	refers back to 1779	MDC 156
,,	17	23 Aug 1731		SRO DD/LW/81

STREET	HOUSE NO.	DATE OF LEASE	COMMENTS	REFERENCE
Selwood Rd	18–19	8 Oct 1753		Frome Museum
,,	29–31	1 May 1690	refers back to 1679	SRO DD/BR/PY Box 5
,,	67	8 Jun 1695		SRO DD/SAS/36/1
,,	76	1725	refers back to 1699	SRO DD/X/NNT/54 C/636
,,	81	28 Aug 1736	refers back to 1729	SRO DD/LW/66 pt 2 of 2
,,	83	28 Aug 1736	refers back to 1726	SRO DD/LW/66 pt 2 of 2
Trinity Row	9	24 Jun 1727	refers back to 1723	JOL 59
Trinity St.	E end. N side	7 Nov 1679		SRO DD/SAS/36/1
,,	,,	30 Sep 1729		SRO DD/SAS/36/2
,,	,,	29 Jan 1772	refers back to 1767	Bristol Baptist College
,,	3	1739	probable identification	SRO DD/SAS/36/2
,,	E end. N side	6 Sep 1746		SRO DD/LW/81
,,	8 S part	27 Sep 1718		JOL 53
,,	8 N part	14 Dec 1743		SRO DD/LW/81
,,	11	25 Sep 1790	refers back to 1779	SRO DD/LW/81 deeds no. 7
,,	18	12 Mar 1723		JOL 58
,,	18	8 Oct 1733		SRO DD/LW/81
,,	20	12 Sep 1774		JOL 20
,,	23	9 Nov 1772	refers back to 1751	Daniel and Cruttwell, Frome
,,	30	5 Mar 1740	refers back to 1727	JOL 16
,,	34	1 Oct 1793	refers back to 1754	JOL 19
,,	35	1 Oct 1790	refers back to 1787	MDC 191
,,	36	19 Sep 1722		JOL 57
,,	37	21 Dec 1805	refers back	JOL 42
,,	39	2 Sep 1760	refers back to 1724	MDC 362
,,	41	25 Mar 1727	probable identification	SRO DD/SAS/36/2
,,	42	23 Jan 1705	refers back to 1692	,, ,, ,,
,,	43	18 May 1693		SRO DD/SAS/36/1
,,	44	29 Oct 1801	refers back to 1750	Frome Museum
,,	46	28 Jun 1788	refers back to 1768	,, ,,
,,	47	10 Oct 1687	probable identification	SRO DD/SAS/36/1
,,	E end. S side	12 Aug 1692	refers back to 1681	WRO 649/10/4
York St.	17	10 May 1688	probable identification	SRO DD/SAS/36/1
Vallis Way	31	20 Oct 1711		SRO DD/SAS/36/2
,,	33–36	10 Mar 1729		SRO DD/BR/fc/24
,,	,,	27 Jun 1750		,, ,, ,,
,,	37	1 Jun 1738	refers back to 1714	SRO DD/SAS/36/2
,,	38 + gap	13 Sep 1726		,, ,, ,,
,,	39 + gap	7 Oct 1738		,, ,, ,,
,,	near 39	3 Aug 1688	see 29–31 Selwood Rd.	SRO DD/SAS/36/1
,,	now lane	9 Nov 1716	between 40–41 refers back to 1667	St John's Frome, churchwardens
,,	41	8 Nov 1716	refers back to 1687	SRO DD/SAS/36/2

APPENDIX 3

GLOSSARY OF STREET NAMES

Badcox   So named in 1605.[1] Called *Seven Dials* in 1810.[2]

Baker St.   Originally a back lane leading from *Selwood Road* to *Naish's St.* and *Vallis Way* before *Selwood Road* was linked directly with *Vallis Way*. Known as *Brandy Lane* by 1785 and renamed *Baker St.* by the Frome UDC in 1904.

Bell Lane   A back lane to lower *Selwood Road* but known as *Bell Lane* by 1753[3]—named after the former Cockey's Bell Foundry there.

Castle St.   Originally the way leading from *Badcox* to *St Katherine's Manor*. The southern part, from the junction with *Trinity St.*, called *Long Row* by 1718.[4] The lower part, northwards from *Trinity St.*, called *Fountain Lane* by 1785 (named after the Lamb and Fountain Inn). The whole street was renamed *Castle Street* by the Frome UDC in 1901 at the request of Messrs Butler & Tanner. (The house on the corner of *Trinity St.* and *Castle St.* was known as 'Castle House' long before becoming the local cottage hospital in 1875.)

A triangular area at the bottom of the street, and nos. 30 to 35 *Castle St.*, were known as *Coward's Batch*.

Duke St.   A continuation of *Naish's St.*, leading to *Welshmill*. In 1805[5] called *Great Katherine St.*, but known as *Duke St.* by 1839.[6] Local tradition links the name with the Duke of Marlborough, the area having been developed soon after his time.

Duke St. Place   Originally called *Kettle* (or *Kittle*) *Alley*, being so named in 1785. Officially named *Duke St. Place* by the UDC in 1897.

Dyer's Close Lane   Described in 1726[7] as the footway leading from Frome to Whatcombe Farm. In church rates called *Dyehouse Close Lane* from 1770 to 1851, and *Dyer's Close Lane* from 1868. In 1821, and for a short time after, the houses on the S side were known as *Peter's Row*. *Catherine Stile* was at the junction with *Milk St.* as mentioned in 1721.

Milk St.   An important way leading from *St Katherine's* to *Whatcombe*. By 1770 known as *Milk St.* A terrace of 4 houses, formerly 3, at the NW corner was designated *Paradise Place* on the 1886 OS map. Further E, adjoining the Rechabite Methodist Chapel, now part of the school, a courtyard was known as *Chapel Court* in 1843.[8] Nos. 16 to 21 *Milk St.* were called *Moxham's Barton* in 1818[9] (they were leased to a Mrs Moxam in 1753).

Mint, The   *Mint St.* used as a name by 1731,[10] and *Mint Sq.* by 1785. Called *The Mint* in 1770. An alternative name was *Middle St.* in 1765.[11]

Naish's St.   The name *Shuttle St.*, usually referring to the E side, was used in 1767[12] and as late as 1844.[13] In 1743 the name *Coombs St.* was used.[14] Known as *Naish's St.* at least since 1785.

Peter St.   In 1765[15] called *Middle Back Lane*, but *Barren Alley* used in 1735[16] and until 1827. In 1828 the name *Peter St.* used.

Pump Lane   A narrow way leading from the W end of *Trinity St.* to *Trinity Row*, so named from 1785.

Rosemary Lane   Not specifically named in 1753, but known as *Rosemary Lane* in 1770. Traditionally part of a herb garden, with *The Mint*, but no evidence has been discovered for this.

Selwood Lane   The southern part, from *Trinity St.* to *Baker St.*, was *Long St.* by 1753, and *Blunt* (or *Blount's*) *St.* in 1751;[17] whilst the northern end was called *Broad St.* in 1753. The whole street renamed *Selwood Road* in 1901 by the UDC at the request of Messrs Butler & Tanner, with their Selwood Printing Works in mind. *The Ope*, obviously an opening, is named in 1785, and refers to a small court on the SW side. In 1881 seven tenements (nos. 22 to 25 Broad St.) were named *The Barracks*, or *Cookes Court*,[18] having been formerly leased by Joseph Cook.

Trinity Row	A footpath leading from Frome to Whatcombe in 1705,[19] but by 1743[20] called *Grope Lane*. Known as *Trinity Row* by 1910.[21]
Trinity St.	The western end, from the junction with *Naish's St.*, originally *Catherine St.* (1722),[22] but called *Trooper St.* in 1772[23] and until 1878 when known as *Trinity St.* (The Trooper Inn is traditionally named after a trooper returned from Marlborough's wars but no proof has been discovered). Holy Trinity Church was completed in 1837. The middle section from *Naish's St.* to *Selwood Road* was known as *Cross St.* in 1687,[24] together with the eastern section. Although a market existed outside The King's Head Inn until 1874, no record of a market cross has been found. The name Cross is therefore probably geographical. The eastern section, from *Selwood Road* to *Castle St.* was originally part of *Cross St.* but by 1770 was known as *Nail St.* (in 1753 a Mr Nayle leased property in the area). The whole street was officially named *Trinity St.* by the Frome UDC in 1901, although it had unofficially been known as such since at least 1854.
Vallis Way	An old established highway from *Frome* to *Vallis*, the home of the lords of the manor. It was named *Vallis Way* in 1671.[25]
Welshmill	Known as such by 1692. *Welshmill Lane* named in 1753.
York St.	Formerly *Milking Barton* (1785) the name *York St.* first occurs in the 1836 rate book.

Unless indicated all dates refer to church rates.
The year 1785 refers to a survey of occupations of heads of households in Frome (Longleat MS WMR Box 29).

1 Longleat MS, WMR Box 29A, 'Froom Westwoodlands. The Perambulation . . .' (1605–6)
2 *Frome Turnpike Act* (1810)
3 Longleat MS, WMR Box 28, 'Survey of Manor of St Katherine's in Frome' (1753)
4 Frome Museum, D72
5 JOL papers, deed 42, in possession of Mr N. F. Maggs, Frome
6 Dobson, *Somerset Directory* (1839)
7 Daniel & Cruttwell, deeds
8 SCC, Ed. 64
9 SCC, Ed. 76/a
10 JOL, deed no. 60
11 JOL, deed no. 52
12 Frome Museum, D66 and D805
13 MDC, D491
14 SRO, SAS/36/2 C61
15 MDC, D426
16 JOL, deed no. 61
17 PRO, C.12/1812/5
18 MDC, D332
19 Daniel & Cruttwell, deeds
20 MDC, D287
21 Frome Electoral Roll (copy in Frome Museum)
22 JOL, deed no. 57
23 Daniel & Cruttwell
24 SRO, DD/SAS/36/1 C61
25 Churchwardens' MSS, St John's Church, Frome

Printed in England for Her Majesty's Stationery Office
by Ebenezer Baylis & Son Ltd, The Trinity Press, Worcester, and London
Dd. 696368 C 35

PLATES

PLATE I

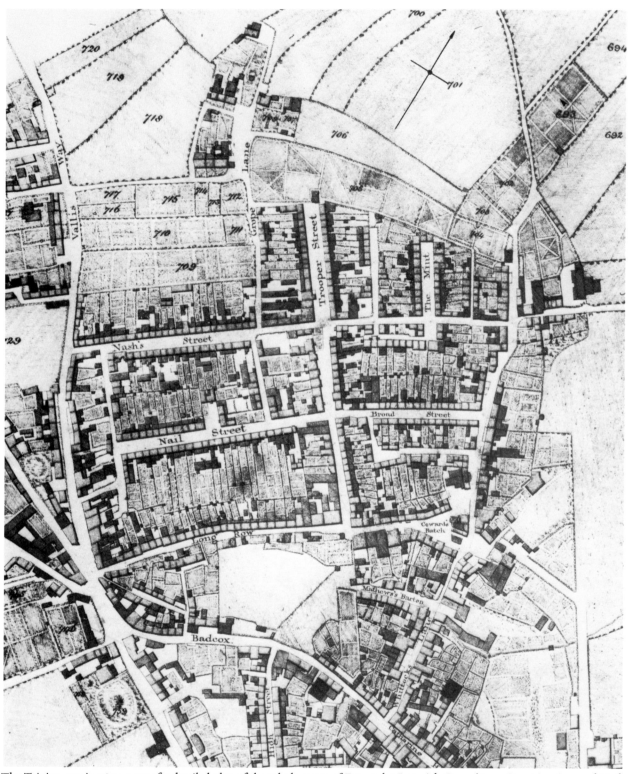

The Trinity area in 1813, part of a detailed plan of the whole town of Frome, by Jeremiah Cruse (Long Street is misnamed Nail Street on the plan). North sign has been superimposed. *Plan reproduced courtesy of the Marquis of Bath. Longleat, Wilts.*

PLATE 2   MID 17TH-CENTURY HOUSES

32–33 Vallis Way, much altered externally and with later fenestration.

48 and 49 Castle Street, the cross-wings added on the street side may be a little later than the main parts of the houses.

1–3 Trinity Street, no. 1 originally with attic gables, built *c*.1680.

The S side of Vallis Way, built without attic gables, *c*.1697.

PLATE 4

EARLY 18TH-CENTURY HOUSES

11 Trinity Street, built with stone-mullioned windows, c.1720.

29 and 30 Naish's Street, built with attic gables in 1705.

PLATE 5

HOUSES WITH STAIRS IN AN EXTERNAL PROJECTION

21 and 22 Selwood Road

STAIRS

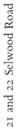

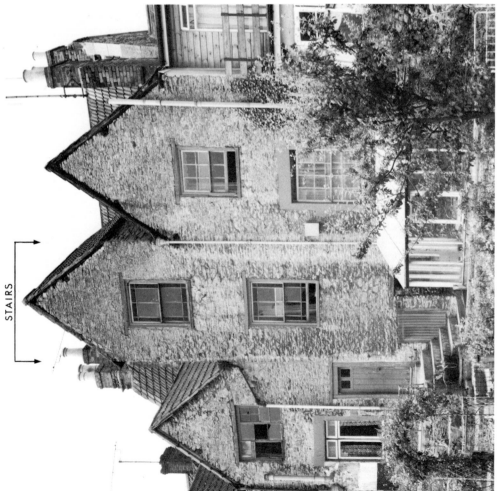

45 Milk Street

PLATE 6   THE USE OF BRICK

7 Trinity Street, cellar of brick with ashlar dressings, *c*.1680.

23 Castle Street, 'The Old Hospital', rebuilt (?) with a brick and ashlar façade in the early 18th century; two of the three attic dormers have been removed.

49 Castle Street, from the rear.

10–14 Naish's Street; heightened and refenestrated in the late 19th century. These are now typical of many late 17th-century houses.

PLATE 8   GROUND-FLOOR ROOMS

39 Vallis Way, built in the mid 17th century; the hall showing the fireplace with an inglenook seat and a plain bressumer over the opening.

7 Trinity Street, built c.1680; the hall showing the fireplace (partly blocked) the axial ceiling-beam (cased) and the ventilated cupboard beside the stack.

73 Selwood Road, late 17th century. The purlins are rough-hewn timbers supported at each end by the gable walls.

39 Naish's Street; the attic floor was always one large room. The roof is of butt-purlin construction.

PLATE 10   WINDOWS

49 Castle Street, mid 17th century, a wooden ovolo-moulded window.

31 Selwood Road, c.1680, a stone ovolo-moulded window with mullions on the first floor (N wall).

19 Selwood Road, late 17th century, a stone window, with chamfered mullions.

21 Castle Street, late 17th century. The landing on the first floor. Morticed into the newel is an original handrail with reeded mouldings.

74 Selwood Road, 1690s winder-stair with moulded risers.

7 Trinity Street, c.1680, framed stairs with moulded risers, the nearer newel ovolo-moulded, the further originally with ball finial.

7 Vallis Way, late 17th century. The winder-stair has moulded risers and is against the stack on the street side.

45 Milk Street, later 17th century; door to one of the attic rooms with decorative hinges and scratch mouldings to stiles and rails.

4 and 5 Naish's Street, c.1692. The doors are to the stairs and two small cupboards beside the stack, a common arrangement.

1 Trinity Street, c.1680, a cupboard beside the stack on the first floor.

20 Selwood Road, late 17th century. Cupboard repositioned in W wall.

16 Trinity Street, *c.*1720. The fireplace has a plain oak bressumer and an inglenook seat. For other typical ground-floor fireplaces see Pl. 8.

1 Trinity Street, *c.*1680. Moulded stone fireplace in the hall, the grandest of 17th-century date recorded. The brick fireback in herringbone bond is surmounted by the matrices for three triangular datestones similar to those at 39 Vallis Way.

PLATE 14   FIREPLACES

39 Vallis Way, mid 17th century. A triangular datestone, originally set above a brick fireback, was found in later rubble infilling. The matrices for similarly inscribed stones were noted at 1 Trinity Street.

2 Trinity Street, c.1680. Chimneypiece on first floor, possibly original. Similar examples have been noted in early 18th-century houses in the Bristol region.

3 Trinity Street. Late 18th-century chimneypiece to hall.

The outline of the original attic gables seen from the E, later built up to form a higher continuous eaves line.

The original end gable in the N wall.

19 Selwood Road, 1680s or early 1690s.

PLATE 16   EXTERIOR DETAILS

5 Vallis Way, 1697. Contemporary with the stone mullioned and transomed window is the oval medallion window lighting the stairs. The original leaded glazing survives.

62 and 63 Naish's Street. The part blocking of earlier windows is visible in the street elevation.

41 and 42 Naish's Street. Straight joints indicate the replacement of wider and shallower windows and successive heightening of the walls.

20 Selwood Road, later 17th century. Bolection-moulded fireplace, possibly contemporary, and shell-niche cupboard.

39 Vallis Way, before *c.*1680. The chamfered ceiling-beam on the ground floor has ogee stops.

45 Milk Street, later 17th century. Oak doors with original hinges survive at attic-floor level.

PLATE 18   STREET VIEWS

Naish's Street from the SW, 1690s. The narrowing at the end of the street reflects former field boundaries.

Castle Street (W side) looking NE. Building continued here until the 1690s.

York Street looking NW. A back lane to Trinity Street, the right hand side was already partly built up by c.1680.

Selwood Road (E side) looking NE. In the distance modern housing extends across the line of former Broad Street.

Trinity Street looking SE. The nearest houses are of the 1720s and later; the gabled houses in the middle distance (nos. 2, 3 and 7) are of c.1680.

PLATE 20   BUILDINGS COMPLETELY OR PARTLY DEMOLISHED

Trinity Street (N side) and Broad Street (W side), all now demolished, and the surviving S side of Trinity Street; oblique views from successive runs of vertical air photographs. *Reproduced courtesy of Somerset County Council.*